CAIRO TRAVEL GUIDE 2023-2024

The Complete Guide to Exploring the City of a Thousand Wonders

Bruce Terry

Bruce Terry

Copyrights © 2023 by Bruce Terry

All rights reserved. No part of this publication may be reproduced, distributed, or transmitted in any form or by any means, including photocopying, recording, or other electronic or mechanical methods, without the prior written permission of the publisher, except in the case of brief quotations embodied in critical reviews and certain other non-commercial uses permitted by copyright law

Bruce Terry

MAP OF CAIRO

Bruce Terry

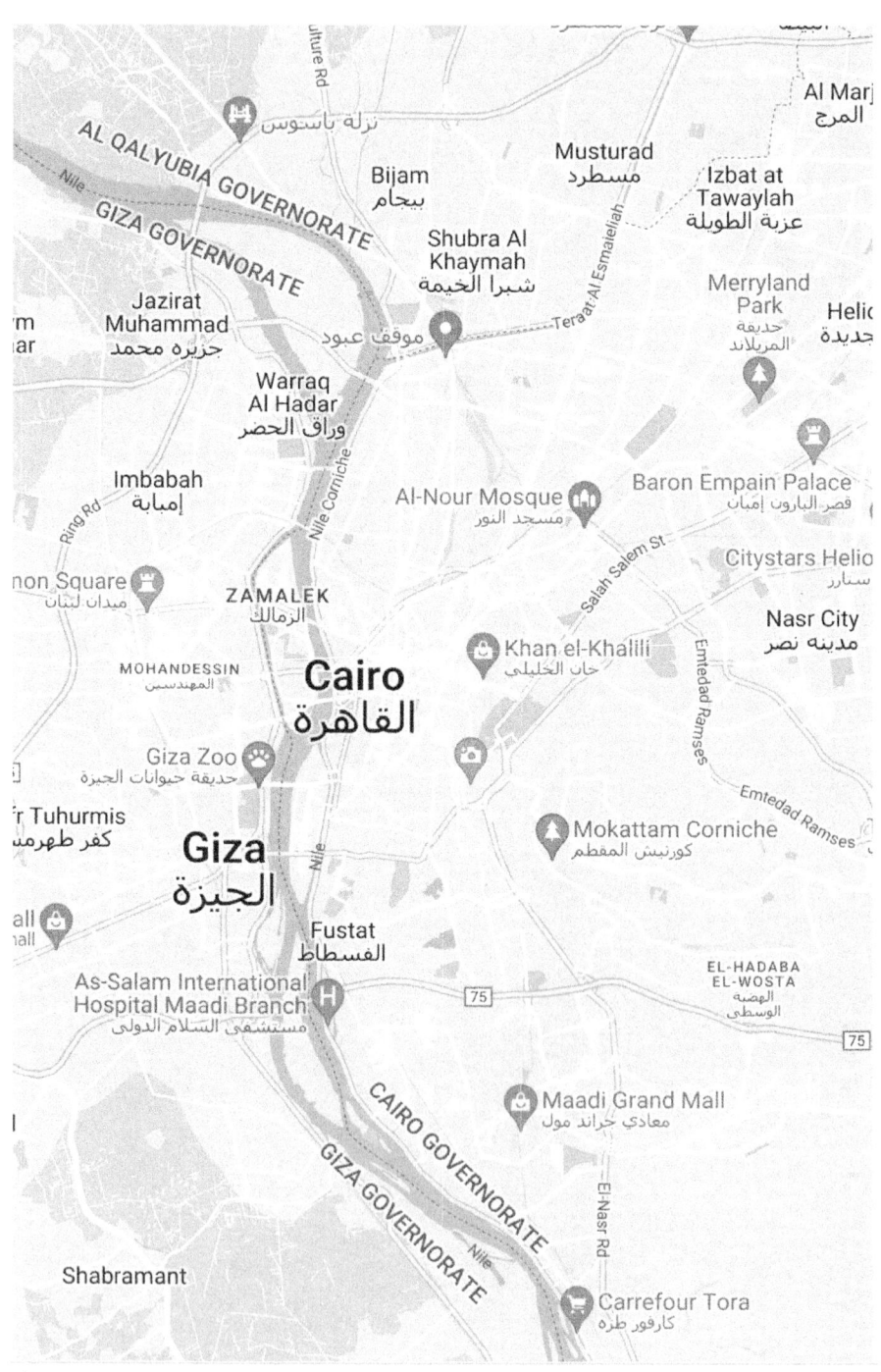

Bruce Terry

Bruce Terry

Bruce Terry

TABLE OF CONTENTS

MAP OF CAIRO 3

INTRODUCTION 11

    HISTORY 13

    GEOGRAPHY 17

    WEATHER AND CLIMATE....................................... 19

    10 REASONS WHY YOU SHOULD VISIT CAIRO 22

CHAPTER 1 25

    GENERAL INFORMATION 25

- POPULATION 25
- PUBLIC HOLIDAY 27
- ELECTRIC PLUG 30
- CURRENCY 33
- LANGUAGE 36
- VISA REQUIREMENTS 38
- DIETARY RESTRICTIONS AND EATING 42
- TRAVEL INSURANCE 46
- CYBER CAFES 51
- TRAVEL PHRASES 54

- LOCAL TIME 57
- CREDIT CARD 60
- ATM 63

CHAPTER 2 67

- BEST TIME TO VISIT CAIRO 67

MONEY-SAVING TIPS WHEN VISITING CAIRO 69

CHAPTER 3 73

GETTING AROUND CAIRO 73

HOW TO GET FROM CAIRO AIRPORT TO CAIRO CITY CENTER 76

HOW TO GET FROM CAIRO AIRPORT TO THE NEAREST HOTELS 80

PUBLIC WIFI AVAILABILITY IN CAIRO 83

CHAPTER 4 89

WHAT YOU NEED TO PACK ON A TRIP TO CAIRO 89

- WHAT TO PACK FOR WINTER 89
- WHAT TO PACK FOR SPRING 92
- WHAT TO PACK FOR SUMMER 95
- WHAT TO PACK FOR AUTUMN 98

CHAPTER 5 103

TOP TOURIST DESTINATIONS IN CAIRO 103

CHAPTER 6 109

BEST BEACHES IN CAIRO 109

BEST RESTAURANTS IN CAIRO 113

BUDGET-FRIENDLY HOTELS IN CAIRO 117

BEST LUXURY HOTELS TO STAY IN CAIRO 122

BEST SHOPPING MALLS IN CAIRO 126

BEST MUSEUMS IN CAIRO 131

BEST PARKS AND GARDENS IN CAIRO 134

BEST NIGHT CLUBS AND BARS IN CAIRO 139

NIGHTLIFE IN CAIRO 143

- ROMANTIC EVENING 143

- LIVE MUSIC 146

FESTIVALS AND EVENTS IN CAIRO 149

HEALTH AND SAFETY IN CAIRO 153

CHAPTER 7 161

FOOD AND DRINK 161

- LOCAL DRINKS 161

- STREET FOODS 166

CHAPTER 8 173

TRAVELING ITINERARY 173

CAIRO TRAVEL ITINERARY FOR 3 DAYS 173

- Day 1: Exploring Ancient Egypt.. 173
- Day 2: Islamic Cairo and Coptic Cairo 175
- Day 3: Modern Cairo and Cultural Experiences.............. 176

CAIRO TRAVEL ITINERARY FOR 7 DAYS 178

- Day 1: Arrival and Exploring Islamic Cairo.................... 178
- Day 2: Giza Plateau and Egyptian Museum 179

CHAPTER 9 183

TRAVELLING TO CAIRO DURING RAMADAN 183

WHAT NOT TO BRING TO CAIRO 186

CONCLUSION 189

Bruce Terry

INTRODUCTION

Welcome to the fascinating city of Cairo, where the echoes of ancient civilizations merge with the energy of contemporary life. As you set foot into this busy city, prepare to embark on a voyage through time, where the past and present meet in a symphony of cultural delights.

From the famous pyramids that have lasted the test of time to the bustling marketplaces packed with scented spices, Cairo is a treasure mine of history, art, and gastronomic pleasures.

As the capital of Egypt, Cairo serves as a portal to the marvels of this great nation. With its strategic position on the banks of the Nile River, Cairo has been a hub of power and culture for ages, bearing witness to the rise and fall of powerful pharaohs, the conquering of empires, and the formation of a modern country. Today, it remains a tribute to the continuing spirit of Egypt, affording tourists an unmatched look into the grandeur of its history and the energy of its present.

No journey to Cairo would be complete without experiencing the fabled Giza Plateau, home to the magnificent Pyramids of Giza, including the majestic Great Pyramid of Khufu. These huge buildings created thousands of years ago, continue to grab the mind with their sheer grandeur and mystery. As you stare at these ancient wonders, you will be transported to a period when pharaohs ruled supreme, and the pyramids stood as an homage to their strength and immortality.

Beyond the pyramids, Cairo uncovers a tapestry of historical and cultural riches. Venture into the heart of the city to discover the labyrinthine lanes of Islamic Cairo, where mosques, madrasas, and mausoleums abound. Lose yourself in the majesty of the Citadel of Saladin, with its massive walls and spectacular views over the city. Step inside the time-honored Khan El Khalili Bazaar, a busy bazaar where the perfume of spices and the music of haggling create an amazing sensory experience.

For those seeking aesthetic and intellectual sustenance, Cairo provides a variety of museums and cultural organizations. Discover the wonders of ancient Egyptian civilization at the Egyptian Museum, home to an awe-inspiring collection of pharaonic antiquities, including the magnificent jewels of Tutankhamun. Immerse yourself in the contemporary art scene at the Cairo Opera House or explore the restored Al-Azhar Park, a verdant sanctuary affording stunning views of the city skyline.

As day fades into night, Cairo comes alive with a dynamic vitality. Indulge in the tastes of Egypt in traditional eateries and street food booths, where delectable meals like koshary, falafel, and shawarma await your taste buds. Experience the busy nighttime scene, where cafés, clubs, and cultural institutions provide entertainment for every choice, from traditional music and dance performances to current electronic sounds.

As you begin your Cairo tour, be ready to be enchanted by its timeless appeal and warm warmth. Whether you are a history aficionado, a cultural expert, or a seeker of unique experiences, Cairo invites you with open arms. Let the city's alluring beauty and rich legacy weave their spell as you make lasting memories in this wonderful place. Cairo, where ancient treasures meet new marvels, awaits your exploration in 2023-2024.

HISTORY

Cairo, the busy capital city of Egypt, has a rich and varied history that extends back thousands of years. From its modest origins as a little village on the banks of the Nile to its reputation as a thriving city, Cairo has been a witness to various civilizations, conquerors, and cultural revolutions. In this essay, we will dig into the enthralling history of Cairo, studying its rise and fall, its architectural marvels, and its crucial role in defining Egypt's past and present.

Ancient Origins: The narrative of Cairo began in the ancient world. The region where the city presently exists was initially occupied some 6,000 years ago, during the Early Dynastic Period of Ancient Egypt. Known as "Memphis" at the time, this early metropolis served as the capital of the Old Kingdom of Egypt and became a center of political, religious, and economic prominence. The city was famed for its large temples, palaces, and the iconic Step Pyramid of Djoser, completed around the 27th century BCE.

Islamic Golden Age: In the 7th century CE, the Arab Islamic conquests swept throughout Egypt, heralding the beginning of a new age for Cairo. In 969 CE, the Fatimid Caliphate erected Al-Qahira (Cairo) as their new capital. Under the Fatimids, Cairo developed as a hub of commerce, learning, and culture. The city underwent a dramatic metamorphosis with the development of large mosques, palaces, and a network of streets and marketplaces that formed the busy core of the city.

The Al-Azhar Mosque: One of Cairo's most prominent structures, was founded during this time. Established in 970 CE, Al-Azhar is one of the oldest colleges in the world and a renowned center for Islamic scholarship, drawing intellectuals from around the Muslim world. The Fatimid period also witnessed the building of the grand Al-Hakim Mosque and the founding of Cairo's famed market neighborhood, Khan el-Khalili.

Mamluk Dominion and Architectural Marvels: In the 13th century, Cairo came under the dominion of the Mamluks, a military caste of slave warriors who rose to power. The Mamluk period is regarded as a golden age for Cairo's architecture, with the creation of spectacular mosques, mausoleums, and palaces that still remain today.

The Sultan Hassan Mosque and the nearby Al-Rifa'i Mosque: both erected during the 14th century, are notable examples of Mamluk architecture. These awe-inspiring constructions display elaborate patterns, towering minarets, and majestic domes, representing the riches and refinement of the Mamluk era.

Another significant Mamluk building is the Cairo Citadel: a large stronghold designed to protect the city. Dominating Cairo's skyline, the Citadel includes various mosques, palaces, and museums, notably the spectacular Mosque of Muhammad Ali, erected in the 19th century.

Ottoman and European Influence: In 1517, Cairo fell under the jurisdiction of the Ottoman Empire, starting a new chapter in the city's history. During the Ottoman rule, Cairo continued to prosper as an important hub of commerce and culture. The Ottomans left their stamp on the city, erecting several mosques, public baths, and other architectural wonders.

However, the late 18th century witnessed the entry of Napoleon Bonaparte and the French troops, establishing an era of European influence in Cairo. Although Napoleon's occupancy was short-lived, it had a lasting influence on the city, spurring a revived

Bruce Terry

interest in Egyptology and ultimately to the translation of the Rosetta stone, a fundamental essential to comprehending ancient Egyptian hieroglyphs.

Modern Cairo: In the 19th and 20th centuries, Cairo underwent enormous transformations and urban expansion. The city's population increased fast, and new neighborhoods, including Garden City and Zamalek, were constructed. Under the British colonial administration, Cairo became the administrative capital of Egypt and a hub for political action.

In the 20th century, Cairo played a major part in the Egyptian Revolution of 1952, which led to the fall of the monarchy and the foundation of a republic. The city continued to develop and modernize, with the building of new infrastructure, universities, and cultural organizations.

Today, Cairo is a thriving city with a population of over 20 million people. It remains the political, cultural, and economic core of Egypt, drawing people from across the globe to discover its historical monuments, thriving marketplaces, and dynamic street life.

Bruce Terry

GEOGRAPHY

Cairo, the capital city of Egypt, is a fascinating metropolis located on the banks of the Nile River in the northeastern section of the nation. With a rich history stretching over thousands of years, Cairo is a city that perfectly integrates old monuments with contemporary advancements. This article will cover the geography of Cairo, diving into its location, physical characteristics, and the influence they have on the city's cultural, economic, and social elements.

Location and Topography: Cairo is situated in the northern portion of Egypt, in the Nile Delta region, which is the lush area where the Nile River fanned out and dumps into the Mediterranean Sea. The city is positioned at the crossroads of Africa, Asia, and Europe, making it a vital cultural and commercial center. Its geographic coordinates are around 30.04°N latitude and 31.24°E longitude.

Nile River: The Nile River, one of the world's longest and most renowned rivers, is a distinguishing aspect of Cairo's topography. As it runs through the city, the Nile separates Cairo into two major sections: East Cairo (the older portion) and West Cairo (the modern part).

The river acts as lifeblood of the city, supplying water for agriculture, transit, and pleasure. It also plays a major part in the

Bruce Terry

city's tourist business, with prominent attractions like the Giza Pyramids lying along its banks.

Urban Development and Development: Cairo has witnessed substantial urban development throughout the years, with the city's population soaring and the metropolitan region extending outwards. This increase has led to the formation of satellite cities, such as 6th of October City and New Cairo, as the city strives to handle the rising population. The urban growth has not been uniformly dispersed, resulting in sharp contrasts between rich neighborhoods and densely inhabited informal communities, known as "ashwa'iyat."

Giza Plateau and the Pyramids: Located on the outskirts of Cairo, the Giza Plateau is a noteworthy geological feature. It is home to the Great Pyramids of Giza, including the renowned Pyramid of Khufu (Cheops), the Pyramid of Khafre (Chephren), and the Pyramid of Menkaure (Mycerinus). These awe-inspiring temples, erected during the Old Kingdom of Old Egypt, are a testimony to the country's old civilization and continue to be prominent tourist attractions.

Environment: Cairo enjoys a hot desert environment, typified by scorching summers and moderate winters. The city gets extremely little rainfall throughout the year, with most precipitation happening during the winter months. Summers are very hot, with temperatures regularly reaching 40°C (104°F), but winters are comparatively warm, with temperatures ranging from 9°C to 19°C (48°F to 66°F). The predominant winds in Cairo are the khamsin winds, hot and dry breezes that blow from the desert.

Environmental issues: As a heavily populated metropolis located in a desert area, Cairo has various environmental issues. Air pollution, produced by car emissions, industrial activity, and the burning of agricultural waste, is a serious concern. The city is also impacted by water shortage, as the rising population limits the existing water supplies. Efforts are being undertaken to solve these difficulties, such as the creation of greener transportation systems and more effective water management measures.

WEATHER AND CLIMATE

Cairo, the capital city of Egypt, is situated in the northeastern region of the nation, along the Nile River. It has a desert climate, which is characterized by hot, dry summers and moderate winters. The city sees varied weather patterns throughout the year, affected by its geographical position and the surrounding desert environment.

Seasonal Variation: Cairo has two primary seasons: a scorching summer and a temperate winter. The summer season spans from May to October, while the winter season lasts from November to April. The transition months of April and November offer weather conditions that might be characterized as a combination of both seasons.

Summer (May to October): During the summer months, Cairo suffers unusually high temperatures. Average daily temperatures vary from 30°C (86°F) to 40°C (104°F), with rare peaks reaching considerably higher. The city is also characterized by high sunshine and little humidity, generating a scorching and dry environment. The evenings are significantly colder, with temperatures falling to approximately 20°C (68°F). Heatwaves are typical throughout this season, and the city regularly experiences dusty or sandy breezes.

Winter (November to April): Cairo's winter season is gentler compared to the sweltering summers. Daytime temperatures vary between 15°C (59°F) and 23°C (73°F), while overnight temperatures may dip to approximately 9°C (48°F). It is the most favorable season to visit the city since the temperature is somewhat cooler and more comfortable.

However, warm gear is still important, especially during the coldest months of December and January. Rainfall is limited throughout the winter, with occasional light showers occurring.

Climate Influences: Cairo's climate is mostly impacted by its closeness to the Sahara Desert and the Mediterranean Sea. The desert, situated to the west, adds to the unusually hot summers and arid weather. The sea, located to the north, has a moderating impact on the city's climate, delivering somewhat milder temperatures throughout summer and mildness in winter.

Sandstorms: Cairo is prone to sandstorms, also known as haboobs, especially during the summer months. These dust storms are created by strong winds moving over the desert, scooping up small sand particles and transporting them toward the city. Sandstorms may impair vision and cause foggy conditions. It is necessary to take measures during such occurrences, including wearing protective gear and masks.

Climate Change: Like many other cities globally, Cairo is also facing the consequences of climate change. Rising temperatures, changes in precipitation patterns, and increased frequency of severe weather events are some of the consequences documented. These changes may have repercussions for agriculture, water resources, and the entire ecosystem.

Bruce Terry

10 REASONS WHY YOU SHOULD VISIT CAIRO

Ancient Egyptian History: Cairo is home to some of the world's most recognizable ancient Egyptian monuments. The Pyramids of Giza, particularly the Great Pyramid of Khufu, are a tribute to the extraordinary architectural accomplishments of the ancient civilization. Exploring these huge ruins and the neighboring Sphinx is an awe-inspiring experience that takes you back to antiquity.

Egyptian Museum: The Egyptian Museum in Cairo is a treasure trove of antiques and antiquities from ancient Egypt. It holds a significant collection of almost 120,000 objects, including the treasures of Tutankhamun. Exploring the museum gives you to experience firsthand the art, jewels, and mummies that provide insights into the ancient civilization's habits and beliefs.

Islamic Architecture: Cairo's Islamic history is reflected in its wonderful architecture. The city is home to numerous spectacular mosques, including the Sultan Hassan Mosque and the Ibn Tulun Mosque. These architectural treasures exhibit elaborate patterns, gorgeous calligraphy, and tranquil courtyards, affording a look into Islamic art and culture.

Coptic Cairo: Coptic Cairo, also known as Old Cairo, is a region that highlights the rich Christian legacy of Egypt. Numerous ancient churches may be found there, including one of Egypt's oldest churches, the Hanging Church (Saint Virgin Mary's Coptic Orthodox Church). You may fully immerse yourself in the history of Christianity in Egypt by exploring this area.

Vibrant Souks & Bazaars: Cairo's busy marketplaces and bazaars give a sensory assault of sights, sounds, and fragrances. Khan El Khalili, the city's most renowned market, is a maze of small lanes packed with stores offering spices, jewelry, textiles, and souvenirs. Exploring these colorful souks is a pleasant experience, allowing a chance to mingle with people and immerse oneself in the local culture.

Nile River: The beautiful Nile River runs through Cairo, giving a lovely background to the metropolis. Embarking on a Nile cruise enables you to experience Cairo's skyline and renowned sights from a unique perspective. You may also take a leisurely felucca boat trip, savoring the serene beauty of the river and its surrounding environment.

Vibrant Nightlife: Cairo's nightlife is noted for its intensity and diversity. The city provides a wealth of entertainment alternatives, including stylish rooftop pubs, lively nightclubs, and live music venues. Whether you want to dance the night away or enjoy a laid-back evening in a nice café, Cairo's dynamic nightlife offers something for everyone.

Bruce Terry

Delicious Egyptian food: Egyptian food is a delightful combination of Middle Eastern, Mediterranean, and North African ingredients. Cairo is a food lover's heaven, providing a vast variety of gastronomic delicacies. From classic street cuisines like koshari and falafel to exquisite Egyptian-style grilled meats and fragrant spices, Cairo's diversified culinary scene will excite your taste buds.

Warm Hospitality: Egyptians are famous for their warm hospitality and welcoming demeanor. Visitors visiting Cairo may expect to be welcomed with real warmth and politeness. The inhabitants are ready to share their culture, customs, and tales, making your stay in Cairo a genuinely unforgettable and enlightening experience.

Contemporary Cosmopolitan Vibes: While Cairo is rich in history, it is also a dynamic, contemporary metropolis with a cosmopolitan environment. The city provides a broad variety of contemporary facilities, including luxury hotels, retail centers, and foreign cuisine. Cairo's combination of the antique and the modern produces a distinct and intriguing environment.

Bruce Terry

CHAPTER 1

GENERAL INFORMATION

- **POPULATION**

Cairo, the huge capital city of Egypt, is not only recognized for its historical monuments like the Pyramids of Giza and the Egyptian Museum but also for its active and varied populace. With a rich history spanning millennia, Cairo has been a cultural melting pot, drawing individuals from diverse regions of Egypt and the globe. In this travel guide, we will dig into the intriguing people of Cairo, studying its variety, customs, and the unique experiences it provides to travelers.

Cairo's Demographics: Cairo is one of the most populated cities in Africa and the Middle East. As of 2021, the expected population of Cairo was over 9.5 million, making it a thriving city. However, the greater metropolitan region, known as Greater Cairo, comprises numerous nearby cities, bringing the population to almost 20 million. The city's fast expansion is a tribute to its economic and cultural prominence in the area.

Cultural Diversity: Cairo's population is a diversified mix of individuals from many origins, producing a unique tapestry of cultures, languages, and customs. The bulk of the population is Egyptian, although you may also meet individuals from several

Bruce Terry

Arab nations, sub-Saharan Africa, Europe, and Asia. The city's global culture gives tourists a chance to witness the confluence of many traditions, cuisines, and art forms.

Historical Influences: Cairo's population has been molded by centuries of historical influences. The city served as the capital of several civilizations, including the Pharaohs, Romans, Arabs, and Ottomans. Each age left its influence on the inhabitants, leading to the diverse tapestry of cultures you see in Cairo today. The architecture, religious customs, and even the local accent reflect this rich historical past.

Neighborhoods and Districts: Cairo is split into several neighborhoods and districts, each with its unique character and population demographics. Zamalek, situated on Gezira Island, is an upmarket district famed for its tree-lined avenues, art galleries, and foreign embassies. Downtown Cairo is the core of the city, with lively marketplaces and historical buildings. Islamic Cairo, often known as Old Cairo, is home to spectacular mosques, ancient architecture, and a dynamic local society.

Street Life and Bazaars: To genuinely feel the populace of Cairo, immerse yourself in the active street life and busy bazaars. Wander around Khan El Khalili, the city's oldest market, where you can mingle with traders, enjoy traditional tea, and bargain for unique items. As you explore the small passageways, you'll discover residents going about their daily routines, creating a dynamic ambiance that displays the city's varied population.

- **PUBLIC HOLIDAY**

When planning a trip to Cairo, it is vital to understand the local public holidays, since they might substantially affect your travel experience. This thorough guide will offer you complete information on public holidays in Cairo, including their importance, cultural festivals, and how they may influence your schedule.

Ramadan (Islamic Lunar Month): One of the most prominent religious observances in Cairo is the month of Ramadan. Although not an official public holiday, it strongly impacts the local lifestyle. During Ramadan, Muslims fast from dawn until sunset, emphasizing self-restraint and spiritual introspection. As a tourist, you should be courteous of this religious practice and abstain from eating, drinking, or smoking in public during daylight hours.

It is a chance to immerse oneself in the local culture by visiting mosques, eating traditional Iftar (breaking of fast) feasts, and seeing the bustling ambiance of late-night marketplaces and streets throughout the festive month.

Eid al-Fitr (Islamic Festival): Eid al-Fitr commemorates the conclusion of Ramadan and is a prominent public holiday in Cairo.

Bruce Terry

The date of this festival fluctuates each year since it follows the Islamic lunar calendar. It is a happy event that lasts for many days, during which Muslims assemble for community prayers, exchange presents, and indulge in feasts.

The city comes alive with bright decorations, exciting street entertainment, and fireworks displays. Many shops, attractions, and government offices may be closed or have restricted hours during this period, so plan your visit appropriately.

Revolution Day: Egypt's Revolution Day, also known as the 25th of January Revolution, celebrates the uprising that took place in 2011, culminating in the ouster of the old president. Celebrated annually on January 25th, this official holiday is honored by different activities, including parades, cultural performances, and meetings in Tahrir Square.

Travelers may experience an atmosphere of solidarity and patriotism among the people during this period. It's crucial to know that certain highways and regions can be restricted due to celebrations, so plan your moves appropriately.

Sinai Liberation Day: Sinai Liberation Day is commemorated on April 25th each year to commemorate the departure of Israeli soldiers from the Sinai Peninsula in 1982. This official holiday is an occasion for Egyptians to exhibit their joy and celebrate the reunification of their country. Festivities can involve military parades, cultural performances, and public activities. If you manage to be in Cairo around this period, you may observe patriotic displays and enjoy the joyful mood.

Coptic Christmas: While Egypt largely follows the Islamic calendar, Coptic Christians celebrate Christmas on January 7th. This holy feast is a significant occasion for the Coptic population in Cairo and is observed by different church services, processions, and festivities. Travelers may visit Coptic churches, such as the Coptic Orthodox Cathedral of St. Mark, to see the vivid celebrations and observe the distinctive Coptic customs.

Conclusion: When planning a trip to Cairo, it is vital to be aware of the public holidays that may affect your travel experience. Understanding the importance of these holidays and their cultural events helps you to immerse yourself in the local customs and observe the vivid spirit of the city. By combining this information into your schedule, you can make the most of your stay in Cairo and create unforgettable encounters. Remember to verify the particular dates and prepare appropriately to ensure that your vacation corresponds with the public holidays in Cairo.

- **ELECTRIC PLUG**

When going to Cairo, the capital city of Egypt, it is vital to be prepared with the appropriate understanding regarding electric plugs and outlets. Understanding the electrical system and plug types helps guarantee that you can charge your gadgets, remain connected, and have a hassle-free vacation. In this tutorial, we will give you extensive information regarding electric plugs in Cairo.

Voltage and Frequency: In Cairo, the usual voltage is 220-240 volts, and the frequency is 50 Hz. This information is vital since it decides whether your equipment will be compatible with the local electrical system. Before connecting any equipment, be sure it can withstand the voltage and frequency used in Egypt.

Most current electronic gadgets, such as computers, cellphones, and camera chargers, are intended to function within this range. However, double-check the voltage rating on your individual equipment or consider utilizing a voltage converter or adapter if required.

Plug Types: In Cairo, the plug type used is the Europlug (Type C) and the Schuko plug (Type F). Let's study these plug kinds in greater detail:

Europlug (Type C): The Europlug is a two-pin plug with two circular prongs, frequently used in most European nations. It has a diameter of 4 mm and is often found in Cairo. The Europlug is compatible with Type C, E, and F outlets. However, it is crucial to remember that not all outlets in Cairo have a grounding connection; therefore equipment that needs grounding may need an adaptor or a different kind of plug.

Schuko Plug (Type F): The Schuko plug is a three-pin plug with two circular pins and a grounding pin. It is extensively used in Germany, Austria, and many other European nations. In Cairo, you may find outlets that take the Schuko plug. If your gadgets have a grounding pin, you may require an adapter or a different kind of plug to utilize them.

Adapters & Converters: If your device's plug is not compatible with the outlets in Cairo, you will need an adapter or converter to guarantee a good connection. Here are some possibilities to consider:

Universal Adapter: A universal adapter is a flexible solution that can support numerous plug types from throughout the globe. It generally has various plug choices and may be changed to accommodate the Europlug (Type C) or Schuko plug (Type F) used in Cairo. It is advisable to get a trustworthy and high-quality universal adapter before your journey.

Bruce Terry

Voltage Converter: If your electronics are not compatible with the 220-240V voltage used in Cairo, you may require a voltage converter. A voltage converter may step up or step down the voltage to fit your device's needs. However, it is vital to remember that not all devices can be used with a voltage converter, thus it is necessary to verify the device specs first.

USB Charging: Another easy method is to depend on USB charging. Many hotels and motels in Cairo feature USB charging connections, enabling you to charge your gadgets immediately via a USB cable. This removes the need for a plug adaptor, but bear in mind that it may not be suited for devices that need greater voltage.

Conclusion: Understanding the electric sockets in Cairo is vital to guarantee you can charge your gadgets and remain connected throughout your vacation. The standard voltage in Cairo is 220-240V, with a frequency of 50 Hz. The generally utilized plug types are the Europlug (Type C) and the Schuko plug (Type F). It is essential to take a universal adapter or the relevant adapters and converters to guarantee compatibility with the local outlets. By being prepared, you can concentrate on enjoying your stay in Cairo without worrying about charging your electronics.

Bruce Terry

- **CURRENCY**

As you plan your journey to this interesting area, it's necessary to educate yourself about the local currency and grasp how to negotiate the monetary environment successfully. In this detailed Cairo travel guide, we'll look into the money used in Cairo, including its denominations, conversion rates, methods of payment, and vital suggestions to guarantee a pleasant financial experience throughout your trip.

Currency Overview: The official currency of Egypt is the Egyptian Pound (EGP). It is indicated by the notation "ج.م" or "E£" and is divisible into smaller units called piastres (pt). One Egyptian Pound is equivalent to 100 piastres. While piastres are still in circulation, the most regularly used banknotes are in denominations of 5, 10, 20, 50, 100, 200, and 500 pounds.

Exchange Rates: Currency exchange rates might vary; therefore it's wise to check the prices before your travel. You may utilize trustworthy currency exchange websites or mobile apps to acquire real-time information. Additionally, banks, exchange offices, and certain hotels in Cairo provide currency exchange services. It's vital to remember that rates could be somewhat better at banks than at exchange offices.

Money Exchange Tips:

Exchange Sufficient Funds: It's advisable to exchange enough money to meet your costs, particularly if you intend to visit places where ATMs or currency exchange facilities may be restricted.

Carry Small Denominations: While bigger shops often take credit cards, smaller sellers and taxis sometimes prefer cash. Having lower denominations of Egyptian Pounds would be advantageous for day-to-day transactions.

Verify Exchange Rates and Commissions: Before converting currencies, check about any commissions or fees associated to ensure you receive the most value for your money.

Save Exchange Receipts: Keep all your exchange receipts. They may be needed for the re-conversion of the remaining Egyptian Pounds at the conclusion of your trip.

Methods of Payment:

Cash is the most generally accepted mode of payment in Cairo, notably in local markets, tiny stores, and street sellers. However, credit and debit cards are accepted at bigger hotels, restaurants, and retail complexes. International cards, such as Visa, MasterCard, and American Express, are frequently accepted, but it's always advisable to carry extra cash for emergencies or instances when cards may not be accepted.

Safety and Security: Exercise care while handling currency in Cairo, as in any other big metropolis. Avoid exhibiting big quantities of money in public and be alert of your surroundings when taking money from ATMs. It's also advisable to utilize ATMs situated inside banks or well-lit regions.

Final Thoughts: Understanding the money utilized in Cairo and its peculiarities can help you negotiate the financial parts of your trip with ease. Be prepared by converting a sufficient quantity of Egyptian Pounds, carrying smaller denominations, and employing credit cards for bigger institutions. With these ideas in mind, you may comfortably explore Cairo's rich cultural legacy, indulge in local cuisine, and immerse yourself in the dynamic atmosphere of this ancient city.

Remember to remain current on conversion rates, retain your currency transaction receipts, and emphasize safety while handling cash. By being prepared, you may completely enjoy the beauty of Cairo while assuring a hassle-free financial experience.

Bruce Terry

- ## LANGUAGE

Learning the local language may tremendously improve your experience and promote meaningful contact with the people. In Cairo, Arabic is the official language, although English is also commonly used, especially in tourist areas. This travel guide will dig into the language of Cairo, including critical information on Arabic, frequent phrases, cultural subtleties, and extra languages used in the city.

Arabic: The Language of Cairo

Arabic serves as the official language of Egypt, including Cairo. While it may seem difficult at first, mastering a few simple Arabic words can dramatically increase your relationships with locals. Arabic in Cairo is predominantly of the Egyptian dialect, which has its distinct pronunciation, vocabulary, and phrases.

English in Cairo

English is frequently spoken in Cairo, notably in tourist areas, hotels, restaurants, and stores. Most persons working in the tourist business have an excellent grasp of English, making it reasonably simple to converse. Street signs, menus, and numerous government papers are also typically accessible in both Arabic and English. However, it's still nice to learn a few Arabic words to show respect for the local culture and create a great impression.

Cultural Nuances in Language

When dealing with locals, it's crucial to be cognizant of cultural differences related to language. Egyptians are typically warm, and welcoming, and enjoy when foreigners try to speak Arabic. Some cultural elements to bear in mind include:

Greetings: Egyptians are famed for their friendliness and like to exchange pleasantries before getting into talks. Taking the time to exchange pleasantries and inquire about one's well-being is considered courteous.

Politeness: Egyptians emphasize politeness, and utilizing expressions like "please" (min fadlak) and "thank you" (shukran) goes a long way in demonstrating respect.

Expressions of thankfulness: Egyptians regularly show thanks with expressions like "Alhamdulillah" (All glory be to God) and "Masha'Allah" (What God has willed), even in daily discussions. It's good to be acquainted with these idioms and utilize them correctly.

Additional Languages Spoken

Apart from Arabic and English, there are additional languages spoken by diverse populations in Cairo. These include:

French: Due to Egypt's historical links with France, French is spoken by certain elderly Egyptians and those working in the hotel business.

Italian: Similarly, Italian is spoken by a limited number of Egyptians, especially in places affected by Italian culture.

Other languages: Due to the cosmopolitan character of Cairo, you may also meet individuals who speak languages like Spanish, German, and Russian, especially in places visited by visitors.

Conclusion: While English is commonly spoken in Cairo, making an effort to learn basic Arabic phrases can immensely improve your trip experience and help you to engage with the local culture on a deeper level. Egyptians love when tourists strive to speak in their original language, and it may lead to more meaningful relationships and memorable encounters. Additionally, being aware of cultural subtleties related to language can help you traverse Cairo's lively streets with confidence and respect. So, pack your

- **VISA REQUIREMENTS**

If you are considering a trip to Cairo, it is vital to educate yourself about the visa requirements to guarantee a smooth and hassle-free voyage. In this thorough Cairo travel guide, we will offer you complete information on visa requirements, including visa kinds, application procedures, and vital suggestions to make your trip experience to Cairo simple.

Visa Types:

a. *Tourist Visa:* This is the most prevalent visa type for people visiting Cairo for tourism reasons. It permits you to remain in Egypt for up to 30 days and is good for a single entrance.

b. *Business Visa:* If you are going to Cairo for business-related activities, like meetings, conferences, or trade exhibits, you will need to apply for a business visa. The time of stay and number of entries may vary depending on your unique needs.

c. *Transit Visa:* If you are transiting through Cairo and have a stopover of more than 48 hours, you may require a transit visa. However, if you are not leaving the transit area of the airport, a transit visa may not be required.

Visa Application Process:

a. *Pre-Application:* Before applying for a visa, confirm that your passport is valid for at least six months beyond your expected stay in Cairo. Also, examine the standards for your individual nationality, since they may change.

b. *Egyptian Embassy/Consulate:* To apply for a visa, contact the closest Egyptian embassy or consulate in your country. Obtain the needed application forms, and assemble the essential documentation, including a completed application form, passport-sized pictures, passport copy, airline itinerary, proof of lodging in Cairo, and evidence of adequate cash for your stay.

c. *Visa charge:* Pay the relevant visa charge, which may vary dependent on the kind of visa and your nationality. Some embassies/consulates may take payment in cash, while others may demand a bank transfer or money order.

d. *Submission and Processing*: Submit your visa application and accompanying documentation to the embassy/consulate in person or via an authorized visa application facility. The processing time might vary, thus it is best to apply well in advance of your trip dates.

e. *Visa Approval:* Once your visa is accepted, retrieve your passport from the embassy/consulate or the authorized visa application office. Verify that all the information on the visa is accurate.

f. *Visa on Arrival:* Some nations are eligible for a visa on arrival at Cairo International Airport. However, it is advisable to secure the required visa before going to prevent any annoyance or delays at the airport.

Bruce Terry

Important Tips:

a. *Plan Ahead:* Begin the visa application procedure well in advance of your trip dates to provide adequate time for processing.

b. *Document Verification:* Double-check all the needed papers before submitting your visa application to prevent any errors or omissions that might lead to delays or denial.

c. *Travel Insurance:* It is important to obtain travel insurance that covers medical emergencies and trip cancellations before going to Cairo or any overseas location.

d. *Extension of Stay:* If you desire to prolong your stay in Cairo beyond the visa validity term, contact the closest Immigration Office in Egypt for information on visa extensions.

Conclusion: Understanding the visa requirements for Cairo is vital for a successful and hassle-free journey. By familiarizing yourself with the visa kinds, application procedure, and vital suggestions included in our Cairo travel guide, you can guarantee that your vacation to this enthralling city is pleasurable and stress-free. Remember to always verify with the Egyptian embassy or consulate in your country for the most up-to-date and correct visa information.

• DIETARY RESTRICTIONS AND EATING

As a traveler, it's necessary to be aware of dietary requirements and navigate the local food scene to guarantee a pleasurable and gratifying gastronomic adventure. Whether you have special dietary restrictions or just wish to explore new cuisines, this guide will help you understand Cairo's culinary culture and identify acceptable alternatives.

Understanding Dietary Limits: Before going on your gastronomic trip in Cairo, it's vital to understand the numerous dietary limitations that may apply to you. Common dietary limitations include:

a. *Vegetarianism:* Vegetarians omit meat, poultry, and fish from their diet but may ingest dairy products and eggs.

b. *Veganism:* Vegans shun all animal products, including meat, poultry, fish, dairy, eggs, and even honey.

c. *Gluten-free:* People with gluten sensitivity or celiac disease must avoid gluten-containing cereals such as wheat, barley, and rye.

d. *Halal:* Halal dietary requirements are observed by Muslims and entail refraining from pork and alcohol while ensuring that meat and poultry originate from animals killed in line with Islamic norms.

e. *Kosher:* Kosher dietary standards, observed by Jewish folks, require precise norms for the preparation and consumption of food, including the separation of meat and dairy items.

f. *Allergies*: Travelers with food allergies should be aware of possible allergens such as nuts, shellfish, and other typical triggers.

Traditional Egyptian food:

Egyptian food is noted for its various tastes, inspired by ancient traditions and nearby Mediterranean and Middle Eastern civilizations. Here are some classic Egyptian foods to try:

a. *Kushari:* A popular vegetarian meal prepared with rice, pasta, lentils, and chickpeas, and topped with tomato sauce and crispy onions.

b. *Falafel:* Deep-fried balls or patties prepared from ground chickpeas or fava beans, frequently eaten with tahini sauce and salad.

c. *Molokhia:* A green leafy vegetable stew often prepared with garlic and eaten over rice or with bread.

d. *Foul Medames:* A typical morning meal prepared with slow-cooked fava beans, seasoned with garlic, lemon juice, and olive oil.

e. *Koshary:* A blend of rice, macaroni, lentils, and chickpeas, topped with spicy tomato sauce and crunchy fried onions.

Navigating Restaurants:

When eating out in Cairo, it's recommended to follow these tips:

a. *Research and plan:* Prioritize investigating places that accept your dietary limitations. Online platforms, travel forums, and local recommendations may be important tools.

b. *Communication:* Learn a few basic Arabic terms relating to your food limitations to assist explain your demands effectively. It's also good to have a written card stating your constraints in Arabic.

c. *Local Cuisine:* Many classic Egyptian foods, such as falafel, hummus, and tabbouleh, are appropriate for vegetarians and vegans. Local street food sellers may give great and economical alternatives.

d. *International Cuisine:* Cairo also provides a large choice of international restaurants catering to diverse dietary concerns, including vegetarian, vegan, gluten-free, and kosher alternatives.

Bruce Terry

Dietary Restrictions and Egyptian Street Cuisine:

Egyptian street cuisine is a must-try experience, but it might provide issues for people with dietary restrictions. Here are some considerations:

a. *Falafel and Ful:* Falafel vendors are prevalent in Cairo, including vegetarian and vegan choices. Full (cooked fava beans) is another popular street food staple suited for vegetarians and vegans.

b. *Shawarma and Kebabs*: While these street food choices are primarily produced with meat, some sellers provide grilled veggie or paneer (cheese) alternatives.

c. *Fresh Juices:* Cairo's streets are dotted with juice booths, selling a range of freshly squeezed fruit juices. Confirm the absence of added sugars or syrups, particularly if you have dietary constraints.

Specialized Dietary Needs:

If you have unique dietary needs such as gluten-free or allergen-free choices, it's suggested to:

a. *Notify in advance:* Informing restaurants and hotels about your dietary preferences ahead of time helps them to make required adjustments and give adequate selections.

b. *Visit health food shops:* Cairo has an increasing number of health food stores where you may purchase gluten-free goods, organic vegetables, and specialist items catering to varied dietary demands.

c. *Use translation apps:* Having translation software on your phone might be beneficial when conveying your dietary restrictions and preferences at restaurants or marketplaces.

Conclusion: Cairo provides a broad gastronomic environment that may suit different dietary requirements. With careful preparation, communication, and study of traditional and foreign cuisines, tourists with dietary restrictions may have a delicious eating experience in this busy Egyptian metropolis. Remember to be open-minded, accept the local cuisine culture, and taste the delicacies that Cairo has to offer.

- **TRAVEL INSURANCE**

To guarantee your vacation is worry-free and protect yourself against unexpected catastrophes, it is necessary to invest in comprehensive travel insurance coverage.

This article serves as a complete guide to understanding the need for a travel insurance while seeing Cairo and emphasizes the essential things to consider when picking the proper policy.

Bruce Terry

I. Why Travel Insurance is Essential for Cairo:

Medical Emergencies: Travel insurance covers coverage for medical expenditures, including hospitalization, emergency medical evacuation, and repatriation. Cairo, like any other location, has its own set of health hazards, and having insurance guarantees you have access to excellent treatment without spending high fees.

Vacation Cancellation or Interruption: Unexpected events such as sickness, natural catastrophes, or political turmoil might compel you to cancel or cut short your vacation. Travel insurance secures your financial investment by reimbursing non-refundable charges such as airplane tickets, hotel, and tour reservations.

Lost or Delayed Baggage: Baggage disasters are not commonplace while traveling. Travel insurance gives coverage for lost, stolen, or delayed luggage, enabling cash to replace critical things and lessen the difficulty caused.

Trip Delays: Flight delays or cancellations might upset your trip plans and lead to unexpected charges. Travel insurance helps cover the expenses of hotel, food, and transportation during such scenarios, so you can continue your travel easily.

Personal Liability: Accidents may happen even during the well-planned travels. Travel insurance includes personal liability coverage, protecting you against legal expenditures in case you cause damage to property or injury to people accidentally.

II. Key Considerations for Choosing Travel Insurance:

Medical Coverage: Ensure your travel insurance covers extensive medical coverage, including emergency medical care, hospitalization, and medical evacuation. Check for pre-existing conditions coverage, as well as coverage for COVID-19-related medical bills.

Trip Cancellation and Interruption Coverage: Look for a policy that covers trip cancellation or interruption due to unanticipated occurrences such as sickness, natural catastrophes, or political upheaval. Check the maximum coverage limit to ensure it fits with your trip expenditures.

Luggage Coverage: Verify the coverage limit for lost, stolen, or delayed luggage. Ensure the coverage covers the worth of your stuff and gives payment for required goods while you wait for your luggage to be retrieved.

Travel Delay Coverage: Confirm the policy's coverage for travel delays, including reimbursement for hotel, food, and transportation expenditures incurred due to delayed or canceled flights.

Emergency aid: Evaluate the emergency aid services given by the insurance provider, such as a 24/7 hotline for medical crises, access to multilingual support, and coordination of medical evacuation if required.

Coverage Exclusions and limits: Thoroughly study and understand the policy's exclusions and limits to prevent any surprises. Common exclusions may include high-risk activities, self-inflicted injuries, or losses due to criminal actions.

Compare quotations: Obtain quotations from several insurance carriers and compare the coverage, benefits, and prices. Choose a policy that best meets your unique requirements and strikes a balance between coverage and price.

III. **Additional Tips for a Safe Trip to Cairo:**

Research Local Laws and Traditions: Familiarize yourself with the local laws, traditions, and cultural sensitivity of Cairo to ensure a courteous and safe vacation.

Be Updated on Travel Advisories: Monitor travel advisories issued by your own country's government or international organizations to be updated about any possible hazards or security problems in Cairo.

Bruce Terry

Take Precautions for Health and Safety: Follow basic safety precautions, such as keeping hydrated, applying sunscreen, and maintaining excellent hygiene. Consider appropriate vaccines and follow COVID-19 safety guidelines.

Keep vital paperwork safe: Safeguard your passport, travel insurance policy paperwork, and other vital documents by saving copies online and retaining physical copies in a safe location.

Conclusion: Travel insurance is a vital component of preparing for your trip to Cairo. From offering coverage for medical emergencies to defending against trip cancellations and lost luggage, travel insurance gives you peace of mind during your vacation. By carefully analyzing the major features described in this book, you can pick a comprehensive travel insurance package that meets your requirements and assures you of a worry-free and joyful trip to see the delights of Cairo. Remember to prioritize your safety, respect local traditions, and keep updated about any travel warnings for a pleasant and wonderful journey in this ancient city.

Bruce Terry

- **CYBER CAFES**

Internet cafés have evolved as attractive venues for residents and visitors alike. These cafes provide a unique combination of traditional Egyptian hospitality with contemporary technical comforts, making them a perfect destination for digital nomads, visitors, and residents seeking a dependable internet connection and a pleasant work atmosphere. In this detailed travel guide, we will cover the greatest internet cafés in Cairo, putting light on their characteristics, locations, and services.

Definition and Purpose of Cyber Cafés: Cyber cafés, also known as internet cafés or gaming centers, are places that allow access to computers, the internet, and different digital services for a price. Originally envisioned as venues for people to browse the internet, cyber cafés have expanded to provide a number of services, including gaming, printing, scanning, and document editing. In Cairo, cyber cafés are regularly visited by students, professionals, gamers, and visitors seeking a dependable internet connection.

Importance of Cyber Cafés in Cairo: Cairo, like any other big metropolis, depends greatly on technology and connection. However, not everyone has access to high-speed internet or a personal computer.

Cyber cafés address this gap by giving inexpensive internet connection and contemporary facilities to those in need. They serve a significant role in supporting Internet communication, research, gaming, and other digital activities. Additionally, computer cafés in Cairo frequently function as social centers, where individuals may meet like-minded people and discuss ideas.

Top Cyber Cafés in Cairo:

a. *The Grid:* Located in the heart of downtown Cairo, The Grid is a popular cyber café noted for its contemporary environment and excellent technology. It provides high-speed internet access, state-of-the-art computers, comfortable chairs, and a variety of tech services. The café also holds gaming competitions and offers a forum for gamers to interact and compete.

b. *Caféspace*: Situated in the Zamalek neighborhood, Caféspace is a renowned internet café that caters to both residents and visitors. It has a comfortable ambiance, with an eclectic blend of antique and modern décor. In addition to internet access, Caféspace offers printing, scanning, and document editing tools. The café also conducts periodic courses and events relating to technology and entrepreneurship.

c. *GameZone:* As the name implies, GameZone is a cyber café largely focused on gaming fans. Located in Nasr City, it provides a broad selection of gaming alternatives, including high-end PCs, game consoles, and virtual reality experiences. GameZone is popular among players seeking a competitive and intense gaming atmosphere.

d. *El-Borg:* Situated in the Maadi area, El-Borg is a well-established cyber café with a dedicated client base. It provides a calm backdrop, making it a great area for work or study. El-Borg offers a variety of services, including internet access, printing, and photocopying. The café also sells a selection of snacks and drinks to keep guests refreshed.

Choosing the Right Cyber Café:

When picking a cyber café in Cairo, consider the following factors:

Location: Choose a café that is conveniently positioned near your hotel or sites you want to visit.

Facilities: Look for a café that has comfortable seats, high-speed internet, and required peripherals such as printers and scanners.

Atmosphere: Consider the ambiance of the café and if it corresponds with your preferences for work or relaxation.

Services: Determine whether the café offers extra services, such as gaming consoles, virtual reality experiences, or refreshments.

Conclusion: Cyber cafés in Cairo provide a combination of contemporary technology and Egyptian hospitality, giving tourists a dependable internet connection and many digital services. Whether you are a digital nomad, a student, or a tourist wishing to interact with others, these cyber cafés offer a friendly and engaging atmosphere. By discovering the greatest cyber cafés in Cairo, travelers may experience the best of both worlds—immersing themselves in the rich history of Egypt while keeping connected to the digital sphere.

- **TRAVEL PHRASES**

It's always helpful to learn a few key phrases in the local language, Arabic. While many Egyptians in Cairo speak English, using a few basic Arabic phrases can go a long way in connecting with the locals, showing respect for their culture, and enhancing your overall travel experience. In this guide, we will provide you with a list of essential travel phrases to help you navigate Cairo with ease.

Greetings and Basic Expressions:

Hello: Marhaba

Good morning: Sabah el-kheir

Good evening: Masaa el-kheir

Thank you: Shukran

Yes: Naam

Bruce Terry

No: Laa

Excuse me: Law samaht

Directions and Transportation:

Where is...?: Fen...?

How much is this?: Bikam dah?

I want to go to...: Ana 'ayez erouh...

Is it far?: Hia ba'eeda?

Left: Yasaar

Right: Yameen

Straight ahead: Ala tool

Dining and Food:

Menu: Al-qaa'ima

Water: Ma'

Tea: Shay

Coffee: Ahwa

Please bring the bill: Min fadlak, ederni el-fatura

Bruce Terry

I'm a vegetarian: Ana nabati

Shopping:

How much does it cost?: Kam sana?

Can you give me a discount?: Momken takhaflee tseer?

Do you accept credit cards?: Hateqbal kardit kredit?

I'm just looking: Ana bas benshoof

I would like to buy...: Ana 'ayez ashtry...

Emergency Situations:

Help: Sa'eeda

I need a doctor: Ana mohtaj tabeeb

Police: Shurta

I lost my passport: Da'afet passsporty

Where is the hospital?: Fen el-mostashfa?

Cultural Etiquette:

Can you help me with Arabic pronunciation?: Momken tesaeedni fi tarteeb el-kalam el-'arabi?

What is this called in Arabic?: Ismoha eh bel-'arabi?

Bruce Terry

Is it customary to tip in Egypt?: Hal m'aroof tazakkar fil-misr?

Remember, when using these phrases, it's essential to approach locals with politeness and respect. Egyptians appreciate the effort to learn their language and culture, and even if your pronunciation is not perfect, they will likely be happy to help you.

Conclusion:

By familiarizing yourself with these essential travel phrases in Cairo, you can enhance your travel experience, interact with locals, and immerse yourself in the vibrant culture of the city. Learning a few key phrases can open doors, create meaningful connections, and show your respect for the local customs. So, pack your bags, practice your Arabic, and get ready to embark on an unforgettable journey through the bustling streets of Cairo.

- **LOCAL TIME**

Knowing the local time not only helps you successfully manage your schedule but also guarantees you make the most of your time experiencing this dynamic and ancient city. In this travel guide, we will go into the nuances of Cairo's local time, including its time zone, daylight saving time, and essential suggestions to bear in mind.

Time Zone: Cairo runs under the Eastern European Time Zone (EET) throughout the year. The time zone is UTC+2, which means it is two hours ahead of Coordinated Universal Time (UTC). This time zone is followed not just in Cairo but also in other major cities of Egypt.

Daylight Saving Time: Egypt does not follow daylight saving time (DST). Unlike several nations that change their clocks forward or backward by one hour during various times of the year, Cairo stays on standard time throughout the year. This absence of DST simplifies the process of keeping track of time, since there are no changes to the local time, making it easier for tourists.

Local Time and Time Difference: Cairo is located in the Eastern European Time Zone (EET) all year round. However, it is vital to be aware of any time discrepancies between your present location and Cairo to prevent misunderstanding and successfully arrange your activities. Here are a few instances of the time difference between Cairo and major cities throughout the world:

London, United Kingdom: Cairo is 2 hours ahead of London (UTC+2).

New York, United States: Cairo is 7 hours ahead of New York (UTC+2).

Sydney, Australia: Cairo is 8 hours behind Sydney (UTC+10).

Bruce Terry

Practical Tips for Managing Local Time:

To make the most of your stay in Cairo, consider the following practical tips:

a. *Set Your Watch:* As soon as you arrive in Cairo, ensure that you adjust your watch or electronic gadgets to the local time. This can help you sync with the local timetable and prevent any misunderstanding with appointments, excursions, or transportation.

b. *Plan Ahead:* Before beginning any activities or trips, make sure to verify the local time. Be careful of opening and closing hours for attractions, museums, and other places of interest, since they may change.

c. *Time Zone Converter:* If you're interacting with people or organizations in various time zones, consider utilizing online time zone converters to precisely organize meetings or conference calls.

d. *Local transit:* Cairo has a well-connected transit system, including buses, taxis, and metro. Be informed of the operation hours and frequency of public transportation to prevent any difficulty when commuting.

e. *Communicating with Locals:* While visiting Cairo, take in mind that locals may refer to the time using the 24-hour clock system.

Bruce Terry

Familiarize yourself with the 24-hour framework to promote successful communication.

Conclusion: Understanding the local time in Cairo is vital for successful travel planning and optimizing your experiences in this interesting city. With Cairo running in the Eastern European Time Zone (EET) throughout the year and without following daylight saving time, you can simply keep track of the local time without worrying about time changes. By setting your watch, preparing ahead, and noting the time difference with your own country, you can make the most of your vacation to Cairo and immerse yourself in its rich history, culture, and exciting environment.

- CREDIT CARD

When it comes to going to Cairo, Egypt, having a trustworthy payment option is vital. Credit cards provide a handy and safe method to control your costs while touring this dynamic and ancient city. In this tutorial, we will dig into the advantages of using credit cards in Cairo, highlight critical concerns, and give valuable recommendations to guarantee a flawless experience.

Benefits of Using Credit Cards in Cairo:

Frequently Accepted: Credit cards, notably Visa and Mastercard, are frequently accepted at major venues, including hotels, restaurants, stores, and tourist sites in Cairo. Carrying a credit card allows you may make payments without worrying about locating an ATM or converting currencies.

Convenience: With a credit card in hand, you may travel lighter by decreasing the need to carry significant quantities of cash. This convenience is particularly significant when visiting busy tourist places where pickpocketing or theft may occur. Moreover, credit cards reduce the burden of frequently transferring currencies, making your purchases swift and efficient.

Enhanced protection: Credit cards give a layer of protection that cash cannot deliver. If your card is lost or stolen, you may immediately report it to your issuer and freeze the account, preventing illegal usage. In addition, many credit card providers have extensive fraud prevention systems in place, affording you piece of mind throughout your travels.

Considerations When Using Credit Cards in Cairo:

Acceptance of Chip-and-PIN Cards: While credit cards with magnetic stripes are accepted at most businesses, it is better to have a chip-and-PIN-enabled card. Some automated kiosks and ticket machines may need a chip-and-PIN card for transactions, notably at metro stations or transit hubs.

Inform Your Bank: Before flying to Cairo, contact your credit card issuer or bank about your trip intentions. This proactive action assures that your card will not be reported for suspicious behavior when used in a foreign nation. Also, enquire about any overseas transaction fees or currency conversion costs to minimize surprises on your bill.

Cash as Backup: While credit cards are routinely accepted, it is nevertheless good to carry some cash as a backup. Although ATMs are generally available in Cairo, they may not be easily accessible in rural locations or during crises. Ensure you have extra Egyptian pounds for little expenditures, tips, and circumstances where cards may not be accepted.

Tips for Using Credit Cards in Cairo:

Informative Signatures: When signing receipts, clearly print your name and cross out any blank places to avoid illegal charges. This method strengthens the security of your credit card transactions.

Local Currency: When given to select between paying in your home currency or the local currency (Egyptian pounds), always go for the local currency. This helps you to avoid costly currency conversion costs and receive the best exchange rate.

Backup Card: Consider carrying an extra credit card or debit card as a backup, held away from your main card. Having an additional payment option is beneficial if your main card is lost, stolen, or refused for any reason.

Bruce Terry

Conclusion: Credit cards offer a simple and safe payment alternative for people visiting Cairo. With global acceptance, greater security features, and the removal of currency conversion problems, credit cards give peace of mind and financial flexibility throughout your stay. Remember to alert your bank, carry some cash as backup, and be careful during purchases to optimize your credit card experience in Cairo.

- **ATM**

When seeing the crowded and ancient city of Cairo, having access to cash is crucial for a comfortable travel experience. One quick and generally accessible alternative for getting local money is via Automated Teller Machines (ATMs). In this thorough guide, we will offer you complete information about using ATMs in Cairo, including their locations, currency exchange choices, fees, and key advice to guarantee a flawless banking experience during your visit to this great city.

ATM Locations: ATMs may be located throughout Cairo, making it reasonably simple to acquire cash whenever required. They are usually situated in banks, retail malls, airports, and important tourist sites.

Some famous banks in Cairo that have an extensive ATM network are the National Bank of Egypt (NBE), Banque Misr, and

Commercial International Bank (CIB). These banks often provide ATMs that accept foreign debit and credit cards.

Currency Exchange: Most ATMs in Cairo give the opportunity to withdraw Egyptian Pounds (EGP) using a foreign debit or credit card. However, it is crucial to know that ATMs mainly dispense local currency, and the conversion rate will depend on your bank or card provider. It is essential to verify with your bank before going to confirm that your card will operate in Egyptian ATMs and to enquire about any international transaction fees or currency conversion costs.

Transaction costs: When using ATMs in Cairo, it is typical to incur transaction costs, particularly if you are using an international card. These costs might vary based on your bank and the sort of account you possess. Some banks may charge a flat fee for each withdrawal, while others may charge a percentage of the amount withdrawn. To minimize surprises, it is advised to enquire about the costs related to overseas ATM withdrawals before your travel.

Security and Safety: While ATMs in Cairo are typically safe to use, it is necessary to take some steps to safeguard your financial information and personal safety. Here are some crucial ideas to consider:

a. Use ATMs situated in well-lit and populated places, such as within banks or retail malls.

b. Be discreet when entering your PIN and cover the keyboard from inquisitive eyes.

c. Inspect the ATM for any suspicious gadgets or manipulation. If anything looks strange, locate another ATM and report it to the bank.

d. Avoid utilizing ATMs that are solitary and placed in secluded regions.

e. If possible, utilize ATMs during daylight hours and avoid withdrawing large sums of cash at once.

Language and Instructions: Most ATMs in Cairo include language choices, including English, to accommodate foreign tourists. However, it is still important to educate oneself with key financial terminology in Arabic to navigate the ATM menus more successfully. If you face any issues, bank workers or other tourists may frequently give help.

Alternative Banking Options: Aside from ATMs, Cairo provides numerous banking choices for acquiring cash. currencies exchange facilities, usually in main tourist destinations and hotels, enable you to exchange foreign currencies for Egyptian Pounds.

Bruce Terry

Additionally, many shops, hotels, and restaurants accept major credit cards, giving you various options for payment.

Conclusion: ATMs are a vital element of every traveler's arsenal while visiting Cairo. With their ubiquitous availability and accessibility, getting cash in the local currency becomes straightforward. By keeping the information offered in this guide in mind, you may successfully navigate the ATMs of Cairo, ensuring you have the required monies to thoroughly enjoy your vacation and see the fascinating attractions of this ancient city.

CHAPTER 2

- **BEST TIME TO VISIT CAIRO**

To make the most of your vacation to Cairo, it's vital to select the perfect time to go. Factors like weather, festivals, and visitor numbers play a key influence in selecting the ideal time to visit this lovely city. In this post, we will look into the numerous seasons and events in Cairo, letting you determine when to organize your amazing vacation.

Weather Overview: Cairo enjoys a desert environment, typified by hot, dry summers and pleasant, somewhat milder winters. Here's a breakdown of the seasons:

Summer (June through August): Summers in Cairo may be sweltering, with temperatures regularly topping 40°C (104°F). The heat may be fairly strong and unpleasant for outdoor activities, making it the least desirable season to visit.

Autumn (September to November): Autumn is a transitional season when the temperatures gradually start to decrease, bringing respite from the summer heat. Daytime temperatures vary from 25°C to 35°C (77°F to 95°F), making it a more comfortable time to explore Cairo.

Bruce Terry

Winter (December to February): Winters in Cairo are warm, with temperatures ranging from 10°C to 20°C (50°F to 68°F). While it may grow cold in the evenings, the moderate weather throughout the day provides for great outdoor touring.

Spring (March to May): Springtime provides beautiful weather to Cairo, with temperatures ranging from 20°C to 30°C (68°F to 86°F). The city flourishes with bright flowers, and the weather is great for viewing ancient monuments and enjoying leisurely walks along the Nile.

Avoiding the Crowds: Cairo is a popular tourist destination throughout the year, but there are occasions when the city enjoys larger visitor numbers. If you like to avoid enormous crowds, it's advisable to stay clear of these busy times:

Winter vacations: The time surrounding Christmas and New Year's, as well as school vacations in Europe and North America, sees a considerable inflow of travelers.

Practical Tips:

Regardless of the time you come, it's vital to carry sunscreen, a hat, and appropriate walking shoes to protect yourself from the sun and negotiate Cairo's congested streets.

Be conscious of Islamic religious practices and dress modestly while visiting holy locations.

Consider reserving lodgings early, particularly during high seasons and events, to ensure your favorite selections.

Conclusion: Choosing the ideal time to visit Cairo relies on your interests in weather, crowd levels, and the desire to enjoy cultural events. Spring (March to May) and fall (September to November) often provide the most pleasant weather and mild visitor numbers. By considering the aspects outlined in this article, you may organize a wonderful vacation to Cairo and immerse yourself in the timeless beauty of this intriguing city.

MONEY-SAVING TIPS WHEN VISITING CAIRO

To get the most out of your vacation, it's critical to monitor your spending. You may enjoy the beauties of Cairo without breaking the bank by using this cost-cutting advice.

Choose an off-peak time to go: Timing is essential if you want to reduce your travel costs. Consider traveling to Cairo between May and September, which is considered the off-peak season, to benefit from cheaper accommodation prices, reduced airfare, and less tourist traffic. Just be mindful of the heat at this time while planning your outside activities.

Bruce Terry

Compare lodging choices: There are many lodging choices in Cairo to accommodate various budgets. Consider alternatives like guesthouses, hostels, or vacation rentals instead of always renting a hotel. You may compare costs and discover economical lodging that suits your requirements using websites and applications like Airbnb, Booking.com, and Hostelworld.

Eat like a native: When visiting Cairo, you must sample the local food, which is also a great way to save costs. Choose neighborhood restaurants and food carts where you may enjoy delectable Egyptian cuisine at affordable costs. Popular and affordable choices include koshari, fuul, shawarma, falafel, and falafel. Be careful to drink enough of Cairo's safe, cost-free tap water to remain hydrated.

Use public transit: Due to Cairo's infamously crowded traffic, it is not only more cost-effective but also faster to depend on public transportation. The Cairo Metro is a practical and reasonably priced transportation option. Buy a rechargeable smart card to save on paying for individual tickets. Another option for finding economical and dependable transportation is to utilize ride-hailing applications like Uber or Careem.

You may save a lot of money by haggling prices, which is a widespread habit in Cairo's marketplaces. Don't be afraid to haggle with the sellers while buying spices, apparel, or mementos in areas like Khan El Khalili or neighborhood markets. When buying many things or in quantity, polite haggling may often result in price reductions.

Discover free or inexpensive activities: Cairo is home to several attractions that won't break the bank. Utilize Al-Azhar Park, the Cairo Opera House, and the Cairo Citadel as free or inexpensive attractions. Visit the well-known Tahrir Square, stroll lazily down the Nile Corniche, or explore the old Islamic Cairo district to experience the city's dynamic atmosphere without breaking the bank.

Buy a tourist pass: If you want to visit many places, think about purchasing a tourist pass. Discounted admission is available to well-known locations including the Egyptian Museum, the Giza Pyramids, and Salah El-Din Citadel with the Cairo Pass or Cairo City Pass. You may also save time by using these passes, which often provide you the ability to bypass the line.

Although guided tours might improve your experience in Cairo, use caution when selecting tour companies. To make sure you're receiving the greatest deal possible, do some advanced research on reliable businesses, compare pricing, and read reviews. Consider group excursions as well as traveling with friends or family to split costs like transportation and guide fees.

Bruce Terry

Conclusion: With the correct preparation and money-saving techniques, visiting Cairo on a tight budget is totally doable. You may enjoy the marvels of Cairo while staying within your budget by choosing off-peak travel times, researching lodging alternatives, delighting in local food, using public transit, haggling rates, visiting free sights, and making wise decisions with tour operators. Without stressing about spending too much money, enjoy your visit to this ancient city.

Bruce Terry

CHAPTER 3

GETTING AROUND CAIRO

Cairo, Egypt's pulsating metropolis, is a fascinating but sometimes difficult place to navigate. Cairo is a huge city with a population of over 20 million people that may be crowded and daunting for visitors. However, getting about the city may be made a lot simpler with careful preparation and knowledge of the various transit alternatives. The several ways to travel about Cairo, including public transit, taxis, ride-hailing services, and walking, will be covered in this guide.

Cairo has a sophisticated public transit system that consists of buses, the metro, and minibuses. The Cairo Metro is a well-liked and effective mode of transportation. There are three lines: Line 1, Line 2, and Line 3, and they jointly cover a large portion of Cairo and its suburbs. The metro runs from early in the morning until midnight, is reasonably priced, and is dependable. However, it may become congested at peak hours, so if at all possible, try to avoid going then.

Another means of transportation in Cairo is via bus, which offers a greater selection of destinations than the metro does. The bus system in Cairo is large, and both state and private bus companies are active there. Buses may be a practical form of transportation, however, they often experience excessive traffic, particularly during rush hours. It's wise to research the routes and timetables beforehand and give additional time in case there are any delays.

Small vehicles that travel along predetermined routes are called minibusses or microbuses. In comparison to other public transit choices, they provide a more flexible and door-to-door service, making them a well-liked means of transportation among residents. Microbuses may sometimes be overcrowded and their drivers have a reputation for driving recklessly, however. If you decide to use this kind of transportation, it is crucial to be cautious and put your safety first.

Taxis: If you want a more direct and individualized transportation experience, taxis are a handy and generally accessible option to move about Cairo. Private cabs are often yellow, whereas official taxis are generally black and white. To guarantee a fair fee, it is recommended to use authorized taxis with functional meters.

Taxis may be located at authorized taxi stops or hailed on the street. To prevent any misconceptions, bargain the price in advance if the meter isn't working. Be warned that Cairo often has traffic congestion, which may lengthen travel times and raise costs.

Ride-Hailing Services: Popular in Cairo, ride-hailing services like Uber and Careem provide a practical substitute for standard taxis.

Through a smartphone app, you may use these services to order a trip and get information about the driver and the anticipated cost upfront. For navigating Cairo's congested streets and securing a dependable and safe form of transportation, ride-hailing services are especially helpful.

Walking: Despite the hectic nature of Cairo's traffic, touring some places on foot may be a good alternative, especially in the city center. You may explore the local culture, take in the sights, and find hidden treasures by walking. Nevertheless, it's crucial to use care and pay attention to your surroundings since pedestrian infrastructure might be inadequate, and crossing busy roadways can be difficult. It's best to stay in busy, well-lit areas while walking, particularly at night.

Additional factors:

Avoid driving when traffic is congested, which is often between 7:30 a.m. and 10:00 a.m. and 4:00 p.m. and 7:00 p.m.

When using public transit, have little change and lesser denomination banknotes with you since drivers may not always have change for bigger ones.

To assist you in navigating and determining the best routes in real time, think about utilizing navigation applications on your smartphone.

Bruce Terry

Be aware of your possessions and take the required security measures to prevent theft and pickpocketing, particularly in busy places.

In conclusion, it takes some preparation and knowledge of the many transit choices to navigate Cairo. It is possible for the public transportation system, which includes the metro, buses, and minibusses, to be successful and affordable. Walking may be an excellent method to explore certain places, while taxis and ride-hailing services provide a more personalized experience. You can travel to Cairo more easily and take advantage of all the city has to offer by taking into account these different forms of transportation and being aware of the city's particular traffic patterns.

HOW TO GET FROM CAIRO AIRPORT TO CAIRO CITY CENTER

Getting from Cairo Airport to Cairo city center is a basic operation, and there are various transit alternatives available to complete this trip. Here's thorough information on how to go from Cairo Airport to Cairo city center:

By cab: Taking a cab is one of the most convenient methods to reach Cairo city center from the airport. Follow these steps:

Upon arriving at Cairo Airport, make your way to the designated taxi area. You will discover well-posted signs or information desks where you may enquire about taxi services.

It is advisable to take the official airport taxis, which are normally colored black and white. These cabs are regulated and regarded as safer and more trustworthy.

Before getting into a taxi, it's essential to negotiate the fee or ask the driver to utilize the meter to guarantee a fair charge. The typical cost for a cab journey to Cairo city center is roughly 150-200 Egyptian pounds (EGP), depending on the traffic and your location inside the city.

Keep in mind that traffic in Cairo may be intense, especially during peak hours, so plan your route appropriately. The length of the taxi travel from the airport to the city center might vary from 30 minutes to an hour.

By Airport Shuttle Bus: Another alternative to reach Cairo city center is by taking the airport shuttle bus service. Here's how to do it:

Upon arriving at Cairo Airport, travel to the airport's bus station, which is situated outside the terminals.

Bruce Terry

Look for the shuttle bus provided by the Cairo Airport Shuttle Bus business. The buses are normally white and orange, and they leave frequently.

The shuttle bus service has multiple routes, including one that travels to downtown Cairo. Confirm with the bus driver or the information desk that you are boarding the proper bus towards the city center.

Pay the fare, which is normally approximately 10-20 EGP, depending on the trip. Keep in mind that you will need Egyptian pounds in cash to buy the ticket.

The shuttle bus travel from Cairo Airport to the city center might take roughly 45 minutes to an hour, depending on traffic conditions and your ultimate location.

By Public Transportation: If you prefer taking public transportation, Cairo also boasts a metro system that links the airport to the city center. Follow these steps to utilize the metro:

Upon arriving at Cairo Airport, find the Airport Terminal 3 metro stop. It is strategically positioned near the airport and gives easy access to the city core.

Purchase a ticket at the metro station. The fare is normally approximately 3-7 EGP, depending on the distance traveled.

Take the metro line 3 (the red line) traveling in either "El Marg" or "Al Ahram" direction, depending on your location inside the city center. It is essential to examine the metro map and plan your journey ahead.

Get out at the relevant metro station in Cairo city center, such as "Nasser," "Sadat," or "Attaba," depending on your location. These stations are strategically positioned and give connections to many regions of the city.

The metro travel from Cairo Airport to the city center normally takes roughly 40-50 minutes.

Important Tips:

It is suggested to carry some Egyptian pounds in cash while commuting from the airport, since not all taxis, shuttle buses, or metro stations take credit cards.

Be aware of possible fraud or overcharging by unlicensed taxis or illegal personnel. Stick to certified taxis or planned transportation providers.

If feasible, get a map application on your smartphone or carry a printed map of Cairo city center to aid find your way to your ultimate destination.

By following these suggestions, you should be able to easily get from Cairo Airport to Cairo city center utilizing a cab, airport shuttle bus, or the metro.

HOW TO GET FROM CAIRO AIRPORT TO THE NEAREST HOTELS

Arriving at Cairo International Airport may be both exhilarating and intimidating, particularly when it comes to finding out the best method to reach your accommodation. In this guide, we will offer you thorough information on different transportation alternatives available, guaranteeing a smooth and hassle-free trip from the airport to the closest hotels in Cairo.

Taxi: Taxis are a popular and handy means of transportation for passengers arriving at Cairo Airport. Follow these instructions to reach your hotel:

a. After departing the airport, proceed to the authorized taxi location.

a. Look for official yellow taxis with meters.

b. Make sure the meter is active at the start of your travel.

c. It is good to have the address and name of your hotel written down in Arabic to show the driver.

g. The taxi price will depend on the distance traveled and the time of day. Ask the driver for an estimated fee before commencing your trip.

Uber/Careem: Ride-hailing services like Uber and Careem are extensively accessible in Cairo and offer a handy alternative to regular taxis. Here's how to utilize them:

a. Download the Uber or Careem app on your smartphone and set up an account if you haven't already.

b. Connect to the airport's Wi-Fi or utilize mobile data to order a ride.

c. Enter your destination (hotel name and location) in the app and confirm the request.

d. The app will show the estimated fee and the driver's data.

e. Follow the app's instructions to locate your driver at the appropriate pickup place.

Airport Shuttle:

Some hotels near Cairo Airport provide shuttle services to take their customers to and from the airport. To employ this service:

a. prior to your arrival, verify with your hotel whether they have an airport shuttle service.

b. If available, enquire about the schedule and any specified pickup sites.

c. Follow the directions supplied by your hotel upon arrival to find the appropriate shuttle pickup spot.

d. Aboard the shuttle and enjoy a quick and straight trip to your accommodation.

Public Transportation: Public transportation options in Cairo include buses and the Cairo Metro. While some solutions may not be as handy with baggage, they are budget-friendly. Here's how to utilize them:

a. Buses: Exit the airport and proceed to the bus stop. Look for buses traveling towards the city center or your preferred location. Remember to bring modest change or an acceptable transit card to pay the price.

b. Cairo Metro: The metro system can be accessed from the airport by taking a bus or taxi to the closest metro station. Follow the indications to buy a ticket, and then board the train traveling towards your destination.

Conclusion: Navigating your way from Cairo Airport to the nearby hotels doesn't have to be a difficult affair. By evaluating the transportation alternatives described above, you may select the one that meets your interests and budget. Whether you select a cab, ride-hailing service, airport shuttle, or public transportation, preparing ahead and being informed of the essential processes will guarantee a smooth and pleasurable trip to your hotel in Cairo.

PUBLIC WIFI AVAILABILITY IN CAIRO

Public WiFi access has become a vital element of contemporary urban life, and the busy metropolis of Cairo, Egypt, is no exception. As the capital and biggest city of Egypt, Cairo provides a wealth of attractions, historical sites, and a bustling environment. The increased availability of public WiFi has altered the way inhabitants and visitors connect to the digital world, promoting communication, accessibility, and convenience. This article digs into the situation of public WiFi in Cairo, analyzing its availability, advantages, restrictions, and advice for safe and efficient use.

Availability of Public WiFi: In recent years, Cairo has experienced great improvement in the creation and accessibility of public WiFi networks. Various organizations, including government authorities, business corporations, and hospitality places, have made measures to construct WiFi hotspots across the city. Key sites where public WiFi is often provided include:

Airports: Cairo International Airport, the principal gateway to Egypt, provides free WiFi connectivity to travelers, enabling them to stay connected while traveling.

Bruce Terry

Hotels and Restaurants: Many hotels, cafés, and restaurants in Cairo give free WiFi access to their visitors, assuring a connected experience throughout their stay or meal.

Shopping Malls: Major shopping complexes and malls in Cairo, including City Stars and Mall of Arabia, provide free WiFi for consumers, allowing them to explore, shop online, or discuss their experiences on social networking platforms.

Public Parks and Gardens: Some of Cairo's prominent public parks and gardens, such as Al-Azhar Park and Al-Azhar Gardens, give WiFi connections to tourists, boosting their leisure experiences.

Government Institutions: Certain government buildings, such as administrative offices and municipal headquarters, provide public WiFi to enable access to government services and information.

Educational Institutions: Many universities, colleges, and educational institutions in Cairo offer WiFi access to students, teachers, and staff, boosting digital learning and research activities.

Benefits of Public WiFi in Cairo: The broad availability of public WiFi in Cairo gives various benefits to residents, visitors, and companies alike:

Bruce Terry

Connectivity and Communication: Public WiFi networks allow users to remain connected, check emails, make video chats, and access social media platforms, boosting communication and decreasing barriers to information.

Tourism & Travel Convenience: WiFi access at airports, hotels, and tourist sites helps passengers to study, plan, and remain connected while experiencing Cairo, boosting their entire experience.

Business and Productivity: Reliable public WiFi helps professionals, freelancers, and entrepreneurs to work remotely, collaborate, and remain productive, converting Cairo into a hotspot for digital nomads.

Access to Information: Public WiFi allows access to educational materials, e-books, news, and online services, empowering people with information and knowledge.

Social Inclusion: The provision of public WiFi bridges the digital divide, ensuring that persons from all socio-economic backgrounds have access to online opportunities and services.

Restrictions and Safety Considerations: While public WiFi in Cairo provides significant convenience, it is vital to be aware of some restrictions and safety precautions:

Security Risks: Public WiFi networks might be exposed to security breaches and data theft. Users should avoid accessing sensitive information or executing financial activities on unprotected networks.

Bandwidth Limitations: Public WiFi networks may face congestion during peak hours, resulting in reduced speeds. Streaming high-definition films or huge downloads may be hard in such cases.

Privacy Concerns: Public WiFi networks may monitor user activities and gather personal data. It is recommended to utilize a virtual private network (VPN) to encrypt internet conversations and safeguard privacy.

Usage Restrictions: Some public WiFi networks may limit access to particular websites or apps owing to content screening or bandwidth management restrictions.

Tips for Safe and Efficient Usage:

To get the most out of public WiFi in Cairo while maintaining safety, consider the following tips:

Use a VPN: Install a reliable VPN program on your device to encrypt your online activity and safeguard your privacy from possible dangers.

Avoid Sensitive Transactions: **Refrain from undertaking financial transactions or accessing sensitive information, such as banking data or personal identity, when connected to public WiFi.**

Enable Two-Factor Authentication: **Activate two-factor authentication for your online accounts to provide an additional layer of protection, minimizing the chance of illegal access.**

Update Software and Apps: **Keep your devices, operating systems, and apps updated to benefit from the latest security updates and bug fixes.**

Be Cautious of Fake Networks: **Verify the validity of public WiFi networks by validating the network name with the institution offering the service. Avoid connecting to networks with questionable or generic names.**

Conclusion: The availability of public WiFi in Cairo has substantially increased in recent years, enabling residents and tourists with seamless access and enriching the city's digital environment. While enjoying the advantages of public WiFi, it is necessary to be cautious, prioritize safety precautions, and make educated judgments about online activity. By harnessing the potential of public WiFi ethically, Cairo continues to develop itself as a connected and lively city in the digital age.

Bruce Terry

CHAPTER 4

WHAT YOU NEED TO PACK ON A TRIP TO CAIRO

• WHAT TO PACK FOR WINTER

Planning a winter vacation to Cairo? While Egypt is famed for its warm environment and blazing summers, winters may be quite cool, particularly during the nights and early mornings. To guarantee your comfort and style, it's crucial to pack the correct apparel and accessories. This extensive guide will help you put together a complete packing list for winter in Cairo, keeping you snug, equipped, and ready to explore this wonderful city.

Layered clothes:

Cairo's winter weather may shift during the day, so carrying layered clothes is crucial. Layering helps you to change your attire according to the changing temperatures. Here are some essential components to incorporate:

a) *Long-sleeved shirts and turtlenecks:* Pack a few lightweight, long-sleeved shirts and turtlenecks that may be worn alone or layered under sweaters or coats.

b) *Sweaters and cardigans:* Carry a range of warm sweaters and cardigans to provide warmth and style to your outfits. Opt for wool or cashmere mixes for extra insulation.

c) Jacket or coat: Bring a medium-weight jacket or coat to protect yourself from cold nights and occasional rain showers. A waterproof or water-resistant alternative is advised.

d) Scarves, gloves, and hats: Don't forget to include accessories like scarves, gloves, and hats. These clothes give additional warmth and shield vulnerable regions from the chilly gusts. Choose fabrics like wool or fleece for optimal insulation.

Bottoms and Footwear:

Ensure your lower body remains warm and comfy by bringing proper bottoms and footwear:

a) Pants and jeans: Pack a variety of jeans, trousers, and comfy pants. Consider thermal-lined choices or layering leggings or thermals beneath your jeans for increased warmth.

b) Skirts and dresses (optional): If you like skirts or dresses, take a couple along with warm tights or leggings to layer beneath.

c) Warm socks: Invest in thick, woolen socks to keep your feet warm. They are especially beneficial if you want to tour outdoor attractions or enjoy a nighttime stroll along the Nile.

d) Closed-toe shoes or boots: Opt for closed-toe shoes or boots that offer insulation and protect your feet from the cold. Comfortable walking shoes are a requirement for touring Cairo's crowded streets and ancient landmarks.

Accessories and Extras:

Don't neglect these crucial accessories and extras that will enrich your winter packing list:

a) *Thermal underwear:* Consider taking thermal shirts and bottoms for additional insulation during exceptionally chilly days or if you intend to visit more northern parts of Egypt.

c) *Sunglasses:* While it's winter, Cairo nevertheless has abundant sunlight. Protect your eyes from the sun's brightness by bringing a pair of sunglasses.

c) *Hand and foot warmers:* If you are extremely sensitive to the cold or intend on spending long hours outside, disposable hand and foot warmers might give further comfort.

d) *Portable umbrella:* Although winter in Cairo is typically dry, it's good to take a compact, collapsible umbrella for unexpected rain showers.

f) *Moisturizer and lip balm:* Cold temperatures may be tough on your skin. Pack moisturizer and lip balm to counteract dryness and keep your skin nourished.

Bruce Terry

Conclusion: Packing for winter in Cairo involves a balance between remaining warm and retaining your sense of style. By following this extensive packing recommendation, you'll be well-prepared to manage the colder weather while seeing the rich history and lively culture of Cairo. Remember to layer your clothes, pick proper footwear, and don't forget the important essentials to make your winter travel a pleasant and memorable experience. Safe travels and enjoy your stay in Cairo!

- **WHAT TO PACK FOR SPRING**

When planning for a trip to Cairo in spring, it's vital to consider the climate and cultural traditions of the city. Spring in Cairo is typically pleasant to warm, with temperatures steadily climbing as the season advances. To ensure you're prepared and comfortable throughout your visit, here is complete and well-explained guidance on what to bring for spring in Cairo:

Light and Breathable clothes: Cairo sees mild temperatures throughout spring, therefore it's best to carry lightweight and breathable clothes. Choose natural textiles such as cotton or linen that enable air circulation and help you keep cool. Opt for loose-fitting tops, t-shirts, and blouses, as well as skirts, shorts, or lightweight trousers. Keep in mind that Egypt is a conservative culture, so it's acceptable to dress modestly, particularly while visiting holy places. Pack a couple of longer-sleeved shirts and long trousers or skirts to protect your shoulders and knees as required.

Layering items: Although spring in Cairo is normally warm, it's always a good idea to carry a few layering items to adjust to variable temperatures. Carry a light sweater or cardigan that you may quickly put on or take off as required. This is especially beneficial during chilly nights or if you want to visit air-conditioned areas like malls, museums, or restaurants.

Comfortable Footwear: Choose comfortable footwear for touring Cairo's streets and sights. Opt for breathable shoes like sandals or open-toe shoes to keep your feet cool. Make sure your footwear is adequate for walking long distances since Cairo is a city best visited on foot. Additionally, carry a pair of lightweight socks for increased comfort.

Sun Protection: With the growing temperatures in spring, it's vital to protect oneself from the sun. Pack a wide-brimmed hat or a cap to shade your face and neck from direct sunlight. Don't forget to carry sunglasses with UV protection to shield your eyes. It's also necessary to carry and consistently apply sunscreen with a high SPF to protect your skin from sunburn.

Lightweight Jacket or Scarf: Although spring in Cairo is normally warm, nights may occasionally be colder. Pack a lightweight jacket or a scarf that you can drape over your shoulders if the weather lowers. This will also come in useful if you want to visit religious locations, where modesty is valued, and you may need to cover your shoulders.

Personal Hygiene Basics: Remember to bring your personal hygiene basics, such as travel-sized toiletries, toothbrushes, toothpaste, and any prescriptions you need. While you can easily find these products in Cairo, it's always helpful to have them readily accessible.

Adapters & Electronics: If you're going from a nation with multiple plug types, ensure you have the right adapters to charge your electrical gadgets. Cairo utilizes the Europlug (Type C) and the Schuko plug (Type F), so make sure you have the proper adapters to keep your gadgets powered.

Travel papers and Money: Don't forget to bring your travel papers, including your passport, visa (if applicable), and any relevant identification. It's also important to have photocopies or digital copies of these papers kept securely in case of loss or theft. Additionally, make sure you have adequate local currency or a dependable way of obtaining cash such as credit cards or prepaid travel cards.

Bruce Terry

Travel Guides and Maps: While you can quickly find maps and information online, it's always nice to have a real travel guide or a map of Cairo. This will help you explore the city, identify attractions, and arrange your schedule more effectively.

Respectful Attire for Religious Places: If you intend to visit religious places such as mosques or churches, it's necessary to dress appropriately. This includes wearing garments that cover your shoulders, upper arms, and knees. Carry a lightweight scarf or shawl that you may use to cover your head or shoulders if necessary.

By considering the weather, cultural norms, and your own tastes, this complete packing list will assist guarantee that you have a comfortable and happy time during your spring vacation to Cairo.

- **WHAT TO PACK FOR SUMMER**

Planning a vacation to Cairo during the hot months? With its blistering heat and diverse cultural experiences, Cairo provides a bustling and interesting summer destination. To guarantee a pleasant and pleasurable vacation, it's vital to pack the correct goods. In this post, we will assist you with what to pack for summer in Cairo, taking into mind the scorching heat, cultural standards, and necessary things for touring and outdoor activities.

Bruce Terry

Lightweight and Breathable Clothing: Cairo enjoys exceptionally hot and dry weather throughout the summer, with temperatures regularly climbing beyond 40 degrees Celsius (104 degrees Fahrenheit). To keep comfortable, bring lightweight and breathable clothing made from natural fibers like cotton or linen. Loose-fitting blouses, T-shirts, shorts, skirts, and dresses are perfect for remaining cool. It's also advised to take a lightweight scarf or shawl to protect your shoulders while visiting sacred places.

Sun Protection: Sunscreen is a must-have item while visiting Cairo during the summer. Choose a high-SPF sunscreen to protect your skin from harsh solar rays. Additionally, carry a wide-brimmed hat or a cap to shade your face and head from harsh sunshine. Sunglasses with UV protection are also vital to protect your eyes from the harsh sun.

Comfy Footwear: Exploring Cairo includes a lot of walking, so it's vital to have comfy footwear. Opt for breathable and supportive shoes or sandals. Closed-toe shoes are advised to protect your feet from dust and heated surfaces. Remember to break in new shoes before your vacation to minimize blisters or pain.

Water Bottle: Staying hydrated is crucial in Cairo's blistering summer heat. Carry a reusable water bottle with you and be sure to drink lots of water throughout the day. It's also a good idea to bring rehydration salts or electrolyte packs to restore critical minerals lost via sweat.

Lightweight Bag: A lightweight and robust backpack or tote bag would come in useful when visiting Cairo. It should be roomy enough to store your needs, such as a water bottle, sunscreen, a scarf, a camera, and any other personal stuff. Ensure it has secure latches to avoid theft and keep your valuables safe.

Modest Clothing for Cultural Places: Cairo is a conservative city, and it's crucial to respect local customs and traditions while visiting religious and cultural places. For these times, carry modest attire that covers your shoulders, arms, and legs. Loose-fitting slacks or long skirts, and blouses with sleeves are ideal. Additionally, packing a light sweater or shawl is essential, since certain interior sites, such as malls or museums, may have air conditioning set at low temperatures.

Electrical Adapters: Cairo, like the rest of Egypt, employs a 220-volt electrical system with Type C and Type F power outlets. If your gadgets utilize a different plug type or voltage, it's necessary to bring the right electrical adapters or converters to charge your electronics securely.

Drugs and First Aid Kit: If you use any prescription drugs, ensure you bring enough supplies for the length of your trip. It's also advisable to take a basic first aid kit that contains necessities like sticky bandages, antiseptic cream, pain medicines, and any special prescriptions you may need.

Conclusion: Packing for summer in Cairo needs careful consideration of the hot weather, cultural standards, and your comfort while seeing the city. Remember to carry lightweight and breathable clothes, sun protection goods, comfortable footwear, and a water bottle. Pay heed to ethnic dress rules and carry modest attire while visiting holy locations. With these basics in your bag, you'll be set to enjoy your summer journey in Cairo while keeping comfortable and respectful of the local traditions.

- **WHAT TO PACK FOR AUTUMN**

When planning for fall in Cairo, it's vital to consider the weather conditions, cultural standards, and activities you want to partake in throughout your visit. Autumn in Cairo normally stretches from September through November, with temperatures progressively decreasing from the blazing summer heat.

To help you pack effectively and enjoy your stay in the Egyptian capital, here is complete and well-explained guidance on what to bring for fall in Cairo:

Clothing:

Light layers: Since fall in Cairo may still be fairly warm during the day, bring lightweight and breathable clothes such as cotton shirts, blouses, and t-shirts. Opt for long-sleeved alternatives for chilly nights.

Cardigans or light jackets: As the temperatures start to drop, it's important to have a light layer like a cardigan or a thin jacket for the nights or chilly days.

Pants and skirts: Pack a variety of long pants and skirts designed from breathable materials. This would give variety for various events and guarantee modesty since Cairo is a conservative city.

Scarves and shawls: These are crucial items to have as they may shield you from the odd cold wind and can also be used to cover your shoulders or head while visiting sacred locations.

Comfortable shoes: Cairo requires a lot of walking, so bring comfortable shoes like sneakers or sandals. Additionally, pack a pair of closed-toe shoes for chilly nights or if you want to attend more formal businesses.

Weather Protection:

Sunscreen and sunglasses: Although October offers cooler temperatures, the sun in Cairo may still be fierce. Protect your skin by bringing sunscreen with a high SPF, and don't forget to bring sunglasses to cover your eyes from the brightness.

Hat or cap: A hat or cap is helpful for added sun protection, particularly if you intend to spend a lot of time outside touring the city or visiting historical places.

Lightweight raincoat or umbrella: Although Cairo sees relatively little rainfall during October, it's always important to be prepared. Pack a lightweight raincoat or a travel-sized umbrella, just in case.

Accessories and Miscellaneous Items:

Power adaptor: Egypt utilizes Type C and F power outlets, so ensure you have the right power adapter to charge your electrical equipment.

Money belt or secure bag: Keep your belongings safe by utilizing a money belt or a secure bag to hold your passport, money, and other vital papers while visiting the city.

Drugs: If you use any prescription drugs, ensure you have an appropriate supply for the length of your stay. It's also good to have a small first-aid kit with basic medical supplies.

Language guide or translation software: While English is spoken in many tourist places, having a language guidebook or translation app might be handy for exploring the city or talking with locals.

Bruce Terry

Cultural Considerations:

Modest clothing: Cairo is a conservative city with Islamic customs, thus it's vital to dress modestly. Avoid apparel that is overexposed or tight-fitting. Women should consider carrying loose-fitting slacks or long skirts and outfits that protect the shoulders and avoid low necklines.

Respectful clothes at religious places: If you want to visit mosques or other religious sites, it's necessary to dress respectfully. Women should carry a scarf to protect their hair, and both men and women should avoid wearing shorts or sleeveless clothing.

Remember to check the particular weather prediction for your trip dates closer to your departure, as weather conditions often alter. By preparing wisely for fall in Cairo, you'll assure a pleasant and pleasurable vacation while respecting the local culture and customs.

Bruce Terry

Bruce Terry

CHAPTER 5

TOP TOURIST DESTINATIONS IN CAIRO

Giza Pyramids and the Sphinx: Undoubtedly the most prominent and recognized sights in Cairo, the Giza Pyramids are a must-visit. These ancient monuments, including the Great Pyramid of Khufu, the Pyramid of Khafre, and the Pyramid of Menkaure, leave tourists in awe at their magnificence. The Sphinx, a majestic statue with the body of a lion and the head of a pharaoh, stands close and completes this extraordinary ensemble.

Egyptian Museum: Located in Tahrir Square, the Egyptian Museum is home to a significant collection of antiquities from ancient Egypt. Visitors may experience thousands of years of history, including riches from Tutankhamun's tomb, mummies, sculptures, and elaborate jewelry.

Salah El-Din Citadel: Situated on a hilltop, the Citadel of Salah El-Din is a historic fortification that gives panoramic views of Cairo. Within the citadel, you'll discover the spectacular Mosque of Muhammad Ali, commonly known as the Alabaster Mosque, which is one of Cairo's most famous structures.

Khan El Khalili: This busy bazaar is a dynamic hive of activity where tourists may immerse themselves in the vivid atmosphere of Cairo. From traditional handicrafts and spices to jewelry and textiles, Khan El Khalili is a great spot to browse for gifts and explore the local culture.

Coptic Cairo: Known as Old Cairo, this neighborhood is home to numerous notable religious structures, including the Hanging Church (Saint Virgin Mary's Coptic Orthodox Church), the Coptic Museum, and the Ben Ezra Synagogue. Exploring Coptic Cairo gives an insight into Egypt's Christian past.

Islamic Cairo: Islamic Cairo is a historic neighborhood that highlights Cairo's Islamic past. The neighborhood is lined with mosques, notably the famed Sultan Hassan Mosque and Al-Rifa'i Mosque. Wandering through the tiny lanes of Islamic Cairo displays breathtaking architecture and a feeling of the city's medieval heritage.

Al-Azhar Park: Located near the historic area, Al-Azhar Park is a calm oasis in the center of hectic Cairo. With beautifully planted gardens, fountains, and spectacular views of the city skyline, this park provides a calm getaway from the city's turmoil.

Nile River: The Nile River is not simply a physical feature but also cultural lifeblood of Egypt. Taking a felucca (traditional sailboat) cruise down the Nile gives a unique view of Cairo and a chance to relax and enjoy the environment.

Cairo Tower: Offering spectacular panoramic views of the city, the Cairo Tower is a famous landmark on the Cairo skyline. Visitors may scale the tower to its observation deck and enjoy spectacular perspectives of the city and the Nile.

Al-Muizz Street: Also known as Al-Muizz li-Din Allah Street, this ancient boulevard is home to some of Cairo's most outstanding Islamic architectural marvels. It is bordered by mosques, mausoleums, and historic monuments, such as the Al-Hakim Mosque and the Qalawun Complex.

Sultan Qalawun Mosque: This 14th-century mosque is one of Cairo's most stunning architectural marvels. Known for its elaborate mosaics, magnificently carved minaret, and spacious courtyard, the Sultan Qalawun Mosque is a must-visit for its historical and artistic importance.

Cairo Opera House: For fans of the arts, the Cairo Opera House is a cultural paradise. The opera house features a range of acts, including ballets, operas, symphonies, and theatrical plays, making it an excellent site to explore Egypt's dynamic cultural scene.

Saqqara: Located on the outskirts of Cairo, Saqqara is an ancient burial cemetery that is home to the famed Step Pyramid of Djoser. This pyramid, dating back to the 27th century BCE, is regarded as

Bruce Terry

one of the first large-scale stone constructions in Egypt and is a UNESCO World Heritage Site.

Memphis: Another historic site near Cairo, Memphis was the ancient capital of Egypt and is now an open-air museum. Visitors may explore the remnants of ancient temples, monuments, and the huge statue of Ramses II.

Al-Azhar Mosque: Founded in 970 AD, Al-Azhar Mosque is one of the oldest colleges in the world and a hub of Islamic study. It's stunning architecture and tranquil ambiance make it a notable religious and cultural monument.

Manial Palace and Museum: Built in the early 20th century, Manial Palace is a beautiful palace complex on Rhoda Island. It shows a combination of architectural styles, including Ottoman, Moorish, and Florentine. The palace presently houses a museum that shows the varied art collection of Prince Mohammed Ali Tewfik.

Cairo Tower: Offering spectacular panoramic views of the city, the Cairo Tower is a famous landmark on the Cairo skyline. Visitors may scale the tower to its observation deck and enjoy spectacular perspectives of the city and the Nile.

Baron Empain Palace: This unusual architectural marvel, situated in the Heliopolis area of Cairo, is an odd combination of Indian,

Cambodian, and French elements. Built-in the early 20th century, the palace is recognized for its distinctive style and lovely grounds.

Al-Azhar Park: Located near the historic area, Al-Azhar Park is a calm oasis in the center of hectic Cairo. With beautifully planted gardens, fountains, and spectacular views of the city skyline, this park provides a calm getaway from the city's turmoil.

Nile Dinner Cruise: A popular way to see Cairo's busy nightlife is to go on a Nile dinner cruise. Enjoy a great lunch while cruising down the river, taking in the brilliant lights of the city's monuments, and enjoying live entertainment.

These 20 tourist spots in Cairo provide a complex tapestry of history, culture, and natural beauty. Whether you're interested in historical treasures, Islamic architecture, or colorful marketplaces, Cairo offers something to enchant every tourist. Explore the city's riches and immerse yourself in its colorful environment for a really unique experience.

Bruce Terry

CHAPTER 6

BEST BEACHES IN CAIRO

Ain Sokhna Beach: Located around 120 kilometers east of Cairo, Ain Sokhna Beach is a favorite weekend escape. Its crystal-clear waters, smooth sandy coastlines, and stunning views of the Red Sea make it a wonderful site for swimming, sunbathing, and water sports.

Ras Sudr Beach: Ras Sudr Beach is a sanctuary for kiteboarding and windsurfing lovers. Its constant breezes, calm waves, and extensive sandy beaches attract guests seeking adrenaline-pumping water sports.

Porto Marina Beach: Situated in the coastal city of El Alamein, Porto Marina Beach provides a magnificent resort experience. Visitors may enjoy beautiful beaches, crystal-clear seas, and a broad choice of attractions, including pools, water parks, and beachfront eateries.

Marina Beach: Located on the North Coast, Marina Beach is a popular location for residents and visitors alike. Its golden dunes, turquoise oceans, and active nightlife scene make it a must-visit place for visitors seeking a dynamic beach experience.

Bruce Terry

Sidi Abdel Rahman Beach: Nestled on Egypt's North Coast, Sidi Abdel Rahman Beach is recognized for its spectacular beauty. The beach's pure white beaches, crystal blue waves, and tranquil environment make an excellent backdrop for relaxing and unwinding.

Ghazala Bay Beach: Situated in the middle of the lovely village of Sidi Abdel Rahman, Ghazala Bay Beach provides a calm respite from the metropolis. Its scenic surroundings, swaying palm trees, and quiet waves make it an ideal setting for a relaxing beach day.

Zafarana Beach: Known for its natural beauty and teeming marine life, Zafarana Beach is a hidden treasure on the Red Sea coast. Snorkelers and divers may explore the beautiful coral reefs and experience a variety of unique fish species.

El Gouna Beach: Located near Hurghada, El Gouna Beach is a gorgeous site famed for its turquoise lagoons and immaculate white sand. The beach provides numerous water sports, such as snorkeling, diving, and sailing, making it a great location for water aficionados.

Golden Beach: Golden Beach is a family-friendly location located in Alexandria. Its shallow seas, well-maintained facilities, and various coastal activities make it a fantastic option for a day's vacation with loved ones.

Amwaj Beach: Amwaj Beach, situated in the resort city of Sidi Abdel Rahman, provides a magnificent beach experience. Visitors may luxuriate in world-class facilities, private cabanas, and gourmet dining selections while enjoying the breathtaking views of the Mediterranean.

Almaza Bay Beach: Nestled on the North Coast, Almaza Bay Beach is recognized for its immaculate sandy shoreline and crystal-clear seas. The beach provides a calm ambiance and a choice of water activities, offering a wonderful beach break.

Zahran Beach: Located in Alexandria, Zahran Beach is a favorite location among residents. It features a large length of sandy shoreline, well-maintained amenities, and lovely Mediterranean air, making it a great destination for relaxing and sunbathing.

Coral Bay Beach: Coral Bay Beach, located near Sharm El Sheikh, is famous for its bright coral reefs and rich marine life. Snorkelers and scuba divers go here to discover the underwater treasures, while beach lovers may rest on the smooth beaches.

Cleopatra Beach: Named after the renowned Egyptian pharaoh, Cleopatra Beach in Marsa Matruh provides spectacular natural beauty. Its turquoise seas, golden dunes, and steep cliffs provide a stunning environment evocative of heaven.

Bruce Terry

Agiba Beach: Located near Marsa Matruh, Agiba Beach is noted for its magnificent cliffs and blue waves. Visitors may enjoy panoramic views from the top of the cliffs, take a plunge in the enticing waters, or just rest on the immaculate sandy beach.

Sahl Hasheesh Beach: Situated near Hurghada, Sahl Hasheesh Beach is a calm paradise with clean seas and a serene ambiance. It provides a variety of aquatic sports, such as snorkeling, diving, and paddleboarding, enabling guests to enjoy the plentiful marine life.

Ras Shitan Beach: Known for its laid-back ambiance and magnificent coral reefs, Ras Shitan Beach is a hidden treasure on the Sinai Peninsula. The beach's easygoing environment, crystal-clear waves, and magnificent sunsets make it an ideal site for a tranquil escape.

Marseilia Beach 4: Located on the North Coast, Marseilia Beach 4 is a popular location for families. Its tranquil seas, sandy beaches, and child-friendly amenities, including playgrounds and water slides, give a fun-filled day for everybody.

Agamy Beach: Situated in Alexandria, Agamy Beach is a vibrant site beloved by residents and visitors alike. Its vast sandy beachfront, lively promenade and bright beach clubs make it a great site for beach parties and social events.

Ras El Bar Beach: Ras El Bar Beach, situated in the Nile Delta, provides a unique beach experience. Its quiet ambiance, breathtaking sunsets, and superb seafood make it a favored destination for leisure and gastronomic pleasures.

Conclusion: Cairo's beaches provide a varied variety of experiences, from calm getaways to bustling beach parties. Whether you're seeking adventure, leisure, or family fun, the 20 greatest beaches in Cairo provide something for everyone. Soak in the sun, feel the sand between your toes, and appreciate the splendor of Egypt's magnificent coastline.

BEST RESTAURANTS IN CAIRO

Sequoia: Situated on the banks of the Nile River, Sequoia provides stunning views and a peaceful ambiance. This premium restaurant specializes in Mediterranean and seafood cuisine, complimented by a well-curated wine list.

Maison Thomas: Established in 1922, Maison Thomas is an iconic Cairo institution. Famous for its pizza and pasta, this Italian restaurant delivers tasty and genuine meals in a lovely, old-world atmosphere.

Kazoku: For aficionados of Japanese food, Kazoku is a must-visit. This trendy restaurant provides a large assortment of sushi, sashimi, and other classic Japanese cuisine, carefully prepared by professional chefs.

Gourmet Burger: As the name implies, Gourmet Burger is a sanctuary for burger fans. With an emphasis on quality ingredients and inventive flavor combinations, they provide a choice of delectable burgers to suit any appetite.

Cairo Kitchen: Dive into genuine Egyptian delicacies at Cairo Kitchen. This restaurant honors traditional Egyptian foods, providing a delightful assortment of mezze, grilled meats, and thick stews, all made with local spices and ingredients.

Taboula: Taboula offers the bright tastes of Lebanese cuisine to Cairo. With a menu that contains a variety of mezze platters, kebabs, and fresh salads, this restaurant delivers an authentic flavor of the Levant.

El Dar Darak: For a unique dining experience, El Dar Darak provides a combination of traditional Egyptian food and entertainment. Enjoy live music and traditional dance performances while tasting tasty Egyptian meals.

Zooba: Zooba highlights Egyptian street cuisine with a contemporary touch. Offering a choice of foods including ta'ameya (Egyptian falafel), koshari (a mixed rice dish), and sandwiches cooked with traditional Egyptian bread, it's a must-visit for foodies.

Kazaz: Indulge in the delicious tastes of Turkish cuisine at Kazaz. This exquisite restaurant provides traditional meals such as kebabs, mezzes, and baklava, all created with painstaking attention to detail.

L'Oriental: As the name implies, L'Oriental provides a gourmet trip through the tastes of the Middle East. With a broad menu offering Moroccan, Lebanese, and Egyptian foods, this restaurant delivers a true sense of the area.

Birdcage: Nestled in the center of Zamalek, Birdcage provides a blend of Asian tastes. From sushi and sashimi to Thai curries and Vietnamese spring rolls, this restaurant amazes customers with its unique and savory meals.

Left Bank: Popular among Cairo's ex-pat population, Left Bank is an elegant brasserie serving a blend of various cuisines. From French classics to American comfort cuisine, their wide menu is guaranteed to impress.

Kazaz: Step into a world of beauty and refinement with Kazaz. With its lavish décor and elegant environment, this restaurant specializes in French cuisine, delivering superb meals and an extensive wine list.

Bruce Terry

Nile Maxim: Embark on a spectacular dining experience onboard the Nile Maxim, a magnificent floating restaurant. Cruising down the Nile, you may enjoy a buffet of different delicacies while taking in the breathtaking views of Cairo's cityscape.

Bua Khao: Bua Khao is a hidden treasure delivering genuine Thai food. With a menu that incorporates classic foods like Pad Thai, Green Curry, and Tom Yum Soup, this intimate restaurant takes customers to the streets of Thailand.

Andrea El Mariouteya: Escape the hustle and bustle of Cairo at Andrea El Mariouteya. Located on the outskirts of the city, this restaurant provides a calm atmosphere and specializes in Egyptian and Mediterranean food.

Le Pacha 1901: Le Pacha 1901 is a floating castle on the Nile River, providing a range of eating alternatives. From exquisite dining at Versailles Restaurant to informal food at The Lemon Tree, this facility caters to all preferences.

Sequoia Beach: A sibling restaurant of Sequoia, Sequoia Beach is a laid-back location set on a sandy beach. Serving a variety of foreign meals and delicious beverages, it's the ideal location to relax and enjoy the sea air.

Kazlak: Kazlak is a fashionable restaurant and lounge that mixes Lebanese and Egyptian cuisines. With its modern atmosphere, live music, and menu showcasing unique fusion foods, it's a popular option for a night out in Cairo.

Le Deck: Situated on the rooftop of the Sofitel Cairo Nile El Gezirah, Le Deck provides panoramic views of the Nile River and Cairo's cityscape. This upmarket restaurant delivers a combination of Mediterranean and international cuisine, backed by a range of exquisite wines.

Conclusion: Cairo's culinary scene is a melting pot of tastes, with a vast choice of restaurants providing varied cuisines from across the globe. Whether you're seeking traditional Egyptian meals, exotic Asian tastes, or worldwide gourmet treats, Cairo offers something to suit every taste. The 20 restaurants featured in this article highlight the finest of Cairo's culinary offerings, assuring an unforgettable dining experience in the heart of Egypt's city.

BUDGET-FRIENDLY HOTELS IN CAIRO

Planning a vacation to Cairo, Egypt, doesn't have to break the bank. Cairo provides a broad choice of budget-friendly hotels that give excellent lodgings at inexpensive pricing. Whether you're a backpacker, a budget-conscious tourist, or just trying to save money on lodging, this guide will introduce you to 20 budget-friendly hotels in Cairo that provide exceptional value for your money.

Bruce Terry

Arabian Nights Hotel: Located in central Cairo, Arabian Nights Hotel provides clean and comfortable rooms at a budget-friendly price. It gives convenient access to major sights such as the Egyptian Museum and Tahrir Square.

Meramees Hostel: Meramees Hostel is a fantastic alternative for budget tourists. Situated near the Egyptian Museum, it provides dormitory-style dormitories and private rooms with minimal facilities, including free Wi-Fi and a shared kitchen.

Freedom Hostel: Conveniently situated near the Khan El Khalili market, Freedom Hostel provides economical private and shared accommodations. The hostel boasts a rooftop patio with great views of Cairo.

My Hotel Hostel: My Hotel Hostel is strategically situated near the major railway station and provides budget-friendly lodgings. The accommodations are clean and comfy, and the staff is nice and helpful.

Cairo Moon Hotel: Cairo Moon Hotel is a nice budget hotel located in the center of Cairo. It provides spacious rooms with contemporary conveniences and a rooftop terrace with magnificent views of the city.

Cecilia Hostel: Cecilia Hostel is situated in the busy area of Zamalek. With its inexpensive dormitory style and private rooms, it gives a pleasant stay near the Nile River and numerous local attractions.

Dahab Hostel: Situated near the Egyptian Museum and Tahrir Square, Dahab Hostel provides budget-friendly lodgings with a welcoming ambiance. The accommodations are clean, and the hostel provides trips to renowned places.

Australian Deluxe Hotel: Australian Deluxe Hotel offers excellent accommodations at an economical price. Located near the Egyptian Museum and the Nile Corniche, it gives convenient access to key sites in Cairo.

Isis Hotel 1 - Downtown: Isis Hotel 1 - Downtown is a cheap hotel situated in downtown Cairo, near Tahrir Square and the Egyptian Museum. It provides clean and pleasant rooms with contemporary conveniences.

City View Hotel Cairo: City View Hotel Cairo is a cheap hotel situated near the Giza Plateau. It provides nice accommodations with air conditioning and free Wi-Fi, coupled with convenient access to the Pyramids of Giza.

New Garden Palace Hotel: New Garden Palace Hotel is located in the bustling area of Zamalek. With its inexpensive rooms and a rooftop patio overlooking the Nile, it offers a delightful stay for budget guests.

Bruce Terry

Cairo Inn: Located in the center of Cairo, Cairo Inn provides budget-friendly lodgings with pleasant and helpful staff. The hotel is within walking distance of significant attractions, including the Egyptian Museum.

King Tut Hostel: King Tut Hostel is a popular alternative for budget tourists owing to its handy location near Tahrir Square and the Egyptian Museum. It provides nice rooms with free Wi-Fi and a 24-hour front desk.

Bella Luna Hotel: Bella Luna Hotel is a modest hotel situated near the Giza Pyramids. It provides clean and pleasant rooms with views of the pyramids, coupled with a rooftop patio and a restaurant.

Hotel Grand Royal: Hotel Grand Royal is conveniently situated in downtown Cairo, providing budget-friendly accommodations with minimal facilities. The hotel gives convenient access to the Egyptian Museum and other key sites.

Tahrir Plaza Hotel: Tahrir Plaza Hotel is located near Tahrir Square and the Egyptian Museum. It provides cheap rooms with contemporary conveniences, including free Wi-Fi and a 24-hour front desk.

Nile Season Hotel: Nile Season Hotel offers budget-friendly rooms along the Nile River. The rooms are pleasant and clean, and the hotel provides a rooftop patio with panoramic views of Cairo.

Hotel Royal Marshal: Hotel Royal Marshal is a cheap hotel situated in central Cairo, near Tahrir Square and the Egyptian Museum. It provides modest and comfortable accommodations at moderate prices.

Nile Zamalek Hotel: Nile Zamalek Hotel is located in the upmarket area of Zamalek. While it offers budget-friendly accommodations, it also includes luxuries like a rooftop pool and a restaurant with Nile views.

Hotel Royal: Hotel Royal is a modest hotel situated near the Giza Pyramids. It provides clean and comfortable rooms with modest facilities, making it a perfect alternative for budget-conscious guests.

Conclusion: Exploring Cairo on a budget is totally achievable given the large choice of budget-friendly hotels available. From downtown Cairo to the Giza Pyramids to Zamalek, these 20 hotels provide excellent rooms at moderate costs. Whether you're a backpacker or a visitor trying to save money, these budget-friendly solutions will guarantee a comfortable and memorable stay in Cairo without breaking the bank.

Bruce Terry

BEST LUXURY HOTELS TO STAY IN CAIRO

For those seeking the ultimate luxury and pleasure throughout their stay, Cairo offers a multitude of magnificent hotels that give unsurpassed comfort and world-class service. In this post, we give a thorough selection of the 20 top luxury hotels in Cairo, where you may enjoy a perfect combination of lavishness and Egyptian charm.

Four Seasons Hotel Cairo at Nile Plaza: Nestled along the famed Nile River, Four Seasons Hotel Cairo at Nile Plaza provides beautiful views and elegant suites. With large accommodations, opulent facilities, and outstanding service, this hotel sets the bar for luxury in Cairo.

The Nile Ritz-Carlton: Located in the heart of downtown Cairo, The Nile Ritz-Carlton is a hallmark of elegance and refinement. The hotel has magnificent suites, a rooftop pool, various dining choices, and a spa, assuring an enjoyable visit.

St. Regis Cairo: Situated along the banks of the Nile, St. Regis Cairo emanates timeless grandeur. With its precisely constructed suites, upmarket dining choices, and gorgeous rooftop pool giving panoramic views, this hotel offers a genuinely opulent stay.

Sofitel Cairo Nile El Gezirah: This five-star hotel blends French art de vivre with Egyptian friendliness. The Sofitel Cairo Nile El

Gezirah boasts nicely designed rooms, a quiet spa, and a range of great eating options.

Fairmont Nile City: Offering a contemporary ambiance and stunning vistas, Fairmont Nile City stands tall as a symbol of modern luxury in Cairo. Its large accommodations, rooftop pool, and superb service make it a favored option for sophisticated tourists.

The Nile Kempinski Hotel Cairo: Nestled in the heart of Garden City, The Nile Kempinski Hotel Cairo exudes timeless beauty. With its spacious accommodations, superb dining choices, and private rooftop pool, it provides a luxury refuge amid the hectic metropolis.

InterContinental Cairo Semiramis: Located on the banks of the Nile, InterContinental Cairo Semiramis delivers a perfect combination of luxury and Egyptian charm. The hotel has contemporary accommodations, a range of dining options, and a magnificent riverbank patio.

Conrad Cairo: Situated in the prominent Zamalek area, Conrad Cairo provides luxury accommodations with panoramic views of the Nile and the city skyline. The hotel provides an abundance of culinary options, a rooftop pool, and a soothing spa.

Bruce Terry

Marriott Mena House, Cairo: Situated at the foot of the Great Pyramids of Giza, Marriott Mena House, Cairo gives a totally unique luxury experience. With its historic beauty, exquisite suites, and lush grounds, this hotel provides a getaway like no other.

JW Marriott Hotel Cairo: Set among beautiful gardens and glistening lakes, JW Marriott Hotel Cairo provides a calm getaway from the city's hustle and bustle. The hotel boasts large accommodations, a championship golf course, and an amazing array of culinary choices.

The Westin Cairo Golf Resort & Spa, Katameya Dunes: Located in the beautiful Katameya Dunes property, The Westin Cairo Golf Resort & Spa is a refuge for leisure and pleasure. With its magnificent suites, large golf course, and soothing spa, it provides a calm refuge away from the city core.

Dusit Thani LakeView Cairo: Nestled in the upmarket New Cairo area, Dusit Thani LakeView Cairo gives a quiet and luxurious experience. The hotel has big accommodations, a magnificent pool, and a range of culinary choices to appeal to every appetite.

Swissôtel Cairo: Situated in the heart of Cairo's commercial sector, Swissôtel Cairo mixes modern style with Swiss hospitality. The hotel has exquisite accommodations, an outdoor pool, and a selection of culinary options to meet sophisticated tastes.

Bruce Terry

Kempinski Nile Hotel Cairo: Overlooking the Nile River, Kempinski Nile Hotel Cairo is associated with refinement and luxury. The hotel features large accommodations, an exquisite spa, and various restaurants providing excellent foreign cuisine.

Renaissance Cairo Mirage City Hotel: Located in the upmarket Mirage City property, Renaissance Cairo Mirage City Hotel provides a sanctuary of luxury and quiet. The hotel has well-appointed suites, a magnificent spa, and a range of eating options.

Le Méridien Cairo Airport: Perfectly positioned for passengers, Le Méridien Cairo Airport is immediately linked to Terminal 3 of Cairo International Airport. The hotel has contemporary accommodations, a rooftop pool, and convenient access to the city's attractions.

Sofitel Cairo Maadi Towers & Casino: Situated in the famous suburb of Maadi, Sofitel Cairo Maadi Towers & Casino provides panoramic views of the Nile and the city. The hotel has beautiful accommodations, a casino, and several dining choices.

Ramses Hilton: Centrally positioned between the Egyptian Museum and the Nile Corniche, Ramses Hilton offers a magnificent getaway in the heart of Cairo. The hotel features well-appointed rooms, a rooftop pool, and a range of eating options.

Bruce Terry

The Gabriel Hotel: Nestled in the upmarket area of Heliopolis, The Gabriel Hotel emanates contemporary elegance and refinement. The hotel has modern rooms, a rooftop pool, and a stylish bar and restaurant.

Le Passage Cairo Hotel & Casino: Conveniently situated near Cairo International Airport, Le Passage Cairo Hotel & Casino provides a blend of elegance and convenience. The hotel has big accommodations, a casino, and several dining choices.

Conclusion: Cairo is a city that exemplifies grandeur and charm, and these 20 luxury hotels reflect the finest of what the city has to offer. Whether you want a Nile-side hideaway, an ancient oasis, or a contemporary urban getaway, Cairo's finest hotels appeal to every taste. With their outstanding service, sumptuous suites, and world-class facilities, these hotels offer an amazing and indulgent stay in the lively capital of Egypt.

BEST SHOPPING MALLS IN CAIRO

Cairo features a booming retail environment with multiple world-class shopping complexes that cater to every shopper's demands. From luxury brands to local shops and entertainment opportunities, these malls provide an exceptional shopping experience. In this post, we give a thorough list of the 20 greatest shopping malls in Cairo, each providing a distinct combination of shopping, food, and entertainment.

CityStars: Located in Heliopolis, CityStars is one of the major malls in Cairo. It offers approximately 750 retailers, including high-end luxury brands, fashion boutiques, gadgets, and more. With a big food court, theatres, and a kids' amusement section, CityStars is a full destination for shopping and leisure.

Mall of Arabia: As the biggest mall in Egypt, Mall of Arabia provides a varied selection of retail possibilities. It provides a broad assortment of local and international brands, along with a variety of food alternatives. The mall also offers an indoor amusement park and an ice-skating rink.

Cairo Festival City Mall: Situated in New Cairo, Cairo Festival City Mall is a prominent shopping destination. It provides a combination of high-end and mid-range retailers, coupled with a large selection of food alternatives. The mall also organizes frequent events and entertainment performances.

Mall of Egypt: Known for its spectacular design and world-class amenities, Mall of Egypt is a premium shopping destination. It contains high-end designer companies, sophisticated eating alternatives, and an indoor ski slope called Ski Egypt.

Dandy Mega Mall: Located in Mohandessin, Dandy Mega Mall is a popular option for both residents and visitors. It provides a broad selection of shops, including fashion, electronics, and home things.

The mall also has a huge food court and a separate space for entertainment.

City Centre Maadi: Situated in the Maadi area, City Centre Maadi is a handy and small mall. It features a variety of businesses, supermarkets, and restaurants, giving a one-stop shopping experience for the people of Maadi.

Sun City Mall: Situated in Heliopolis, Sun City Mall is a contemporary and elegant retail destination. It contains a broad mix of local and international businesses, coupled with leisure alternatives including a cinema complex and a family amusement center.

Point 90 Mall: Located in New Cairo, Point 90 Mall provides a unique shopping experience. It features a range of fashionable stores, elegant restaurants, and a big outdoor space suitable for mingling and resting.

The District Mall: Situated in the heart of Sheikh Zayed City, The District Mall is a sleek and sophisticated retail destination. It features high-end retail outlets, sophisticated eating alternatives, and a variety of entertainment amenities.

Genena Mall: Located in Nasr City, Genena Mall is a popular retail mall. It contains a range of retailers, including fashion, electronics, and home goods. The mall also provides a number of culinary alternatives, making it a popular place for residents.

Arkadia Mall: Situated in Madinaty, Arkadia Mall is a family-friendly shopping attraction. It provides a mix of local and international brands, along with leisure choices such as a multiplex theatre and a specialized play area for children.

Downtown Mall: Located in New Cairo, Downtown Mall stands out for its modern architecture and upmarket retail experience. It provides a mix of premium goods, exquisite dining choices, and a rooftop patio with panoramic views.

Porto Cairo Mall: Situated in New Cairo, Porto Cairo Mall is a popular retail attraction. It provides a large choice of stores, restaurants, and entertainment opportunities, including a bowling alley and a movie complex.

Tivoli Dome: Located in Heliopolis, Tivoli Dome is a unique retail and entertainment complex. It contains an assortment of boutiques, restaurants, and cafés, along with a big outdoor area for events and live performances.

CFC Mall: Situated in the Fifth Settlement, CFC Mall provides a varied choice of retail and eating alternatives. It offers a mix of local and international brands, together with a huge food court and a designated space for kids' activities.

Bruce Terry

Festival City Mall: Located in New Cairo, Festival City Mall is a popular destination for consumers. It contains a combination of well-known companies, stylish shops, and a variety of food alternatives. The mall also offers frequent events and exhibits.

Cairo Festival Plaza: Situated in the Fifth Settlement, Cairo Festival Plaza is a sophisticated retail attraction. It includes a large choice of boutiques, restaurants, and cafés, along with a specific section for kids' amusement.

Royal Maxim Palace Kempinski Mall: Located in New Cairo, this mall is part of the opulent Royal Maxim Palace Kempinski Hotel. It provides an outstanding range of premium goods, coupled with upmarket eating choices and a spa.

First Mall: Situated in Giza, First Mall is a high-end retail attraction. It is noted for its exclusive luxury stores, great eating places, and breathtaking views of the Nile River.

Golden Eagle Mall: Located in Nasr City, Golden Eagle Mall provides a mix of local and international brands. It contains a range of stores, a food court, and entertainment alternatives such as a movie complex.

Conclusion: Cairo's retail malls provide a wealth of alternatives for any customer, from premium brands to economical apparel, gadgets, and food choices. Whether you're a local resident or a visitor, these malls offer a wonderful shopping experience, combined with entertainment opportunities to appeal to all interests. Embark on a retail expedition and discover the different options of Cairo's 20 greatest shopping malls for an amazing experience.

BEST MUSEUMS IN CAIRO

Cairo's museums provide a fascinating trip through antiquity. In this post, we will examine the 20 top museums in Cairo, emphasizing their distinct collections and historical relevance.

Egyptian Museum: Located in Tahrir Square, the Egyptian Museum is one of the most important museums in the world. It holds a vast collection of ancient Egyptian antiquities, including the famed treasures of Tutankhamun, mummies, sculptures, and hieroglyphics.

Gayer-Anderson Museum: Situated in the heart of Islamic Cairo, this museum is named after Major R.G. Gayer-Anderson, who resided in the home and gathered a wonderful assortment of Islamic art and antiquities. It shows wonderfully designed rooms, furniture, rugs, and manuscripts.

Museum of Islamic Art: Located in Bab al-Khalq, this museum is devoted to Islamic art and culture. It has a huge collection of antiquities, including pottery, metalwork, textiles, and rare Qur'ans, spanning many centuries.

Coptic Museum: Situated in Old Cairo, the Coptic Museum showcases a vast collection of Coptic Christian art, including icons, manuscripts, textiles, and architectural remains, offering insight into Egypt's Christian legacy.

Museum of Egyptian Contemporary Arts: This museum, located in Gezira, shows the works of notable Egyptian contemporary artists. It contains diverse creative genres and materials, including paintings, sculptures, and installations.

Manial Palace Museum: Located on Rhoda Island, the Manial Palace Museum gives an insight into the life of Prince Mohammed Ali Tewfik and his diverse taste. It has a wide collection of art, furniture, pottery, and manuscripts.

Museum of Islamic Ceramics: Situated in Al-Darb al-Ahmar, this museum shows a vast variety of Islamic ceramics, including tiles, pottery, and ornamental artifacts. The collection reflects diverse eras and styles of Islamic pottery.

Museum of Islamic Textiles: Located on Al-Muizz Street, this museum shows a unique collection of Islamic textiles, including carpets, clothing, and tapestries. Visitors may examine the complex patterns and brilliant hues of these masterpieces.

Bruce Terry

The National Museum of Egyptian Civilization: This recently established museum in Fustat presents a thorough picture of Egyptian civilization from ancient times to the current day. It offers exhibits on ancient Egypt, the Greco-Roman period, the Coptic and Islamic periods, and current Egyptian history.

Mohamed Mahmoud Khalil Museum: Situated in Giza: this museum holds the private collection of Mohamed Mahmoud Khalil, a notable Egyptian politician and art collector. It shows a magnificent collection of European and Egyptian art, including pieces by Van Gogh, Monet, and Matisse.

The Royal Jewels Museum: Located in Alexandria, a short distance from Cairo, this museum shows an outstanding collection of jewels belonging to the royal family of Egypt. Visitors may view beautiful tiaras, necklaces, and other expensive stones.

The Museum of Islamic Civilization: Situated in Sharjah City, this museum highlights Islamic art and culture via interactive exhibitions and multimedia presentations. It displays artifacts from many countries and chronological eras, presenting a thorough overview of Islamic civilization.

Bruce Terry

BEST PARKS AND GARDENS IN CAIRO

Cairo is also home to some gorgeous parks and gardens that give a getaway from the fast-paced daily life. These green oases offer a refreshing getaway, enabling visitors to rest, relax, and immerse themselves in nature's splendor. In this post, we will examine the 20 greatest parks and gardens in Cairo, each giving a distinct experience and an insight into the city's natural side.

Al-Azhar Park: Located in the center of Old Cairo, Al-Azhar Park is a beautifully designed park stretching over 30 acres. The park includes lovely gardens, fountains, and great views of the old city. It also has various old buildings, a lake, and a children's playground.

Al-Andalus Park: Situated in the Zamalek area, Al-Andalus Park is recognized for its stunning Andalusian-inspired architecture and lush flora. Visitors may enjoy strolling walkways, beautiful flowers, shaded seats, and breathtaking views of the Nile River.

Orman Botanical Garden: Established in 1875, the Orman Botanical Garden is Egypt's oldest botanical garden. It shows a wide array of plants, including uncommon species, tall trees, and vivid flowers. The garden contains quiet ponds, lovely gazebos, and picnic spaces.

International Park: Located in Nasr City, the International Park is a popular leisure destination with huge open spaces, gorgeous gardens, and walking routes. It provides many activities, including boating, horse riding, and cycling, making it a perfect vacation for families.

Gezira Club Park: Situated on Gezira Island, the Gezira Club Park is a gorgeous park encircled by the Nile River. The park offers well-maintained grass, recreational facilities, picnic spots, and a small zoo. Visitors may also enjoy boat rides on the river.

Cairo Opera House Grounds: Nestled in the middle of the city, the Cairo Opera House Grounds provide a quiet setting with groomed lawns, unique sculptures, and gorgeous flower beds. The park is a favored area for walkers, joggers, and people seeking a moment of peace.

Aquarium Grotto Garden: Located in Heliopolis, the Aquarium Grotto Garden is a lovely park with lush flora, peaceful water features, and a cave-like structure containing an aquarium. It is a fantastic area for a leisurely walk or a family picnic.

Al-Azhar Park Extension: Adjacent to the original Al-Azhar Park, the Al-Azhar Park Extension includes additional green areas, botanical gardens, and pathways. It gives tourists a calm ambiance and spectacular views of the park and the city skyline.

Bruce Terry

Family Park: Situated in New Cairo, the Family Park is a big park with extensive grassy spaces, playgrounds, and sports facilities. It is a popular area for families to relax, engage in outdoor activities, and have picnics in a pleasant ambiance.

Al-Orman Park: Al-Orman Park, situated near Giza, is a huge green park that provides a broad variety of leisure activities. It offers tree-lined streets, magnificent gardens, a boating lake, and horse riding facilities. The park regularly holds cultural events and festivals.

Giza Zoo: Established in 1891, the Giza Zoo is one of the oldest and biggest zoos in Africa. It encompasses over 80 acres and is home to a wide array of animals and birds. The zoo's beautiful environs make it an ideal spot to spend a day exploring nature.

Al-Azhar Park Amphitheatre: Situated inside Al-Azhar Park, the Amphitheatre accommodates numerous cultural events, including live performances, concerts, and theatrical presentations. The wonderfully built outdoor theater gives a unique experience where guests may enjoy entertainment surrounded by natural beauty.

Al-Jazira Park: Located in the Maadi neighborhood, Al-Jazira Park is a popular leisure facility containing open green spaces, jogging tracks, sports courts, and children's play areas. The park's calm environment draws residents and visitors alike.

Bruce Terry

Al-Azhar Park Lake: Set within the gorgeous surroundings of Al-Azhar Park, the lake provides a calm getaway where tourists may enjoy boat rides and view the park's rich foliage. The lake is a tranquil area, great for couples, families, or anyone seeking leisure.

Al-Andalus Garden Park: Situated in the Heliopolis neighborhood, Al-Andalus Garden Park is noted for its spectacular landscape design influenced by Andalusian gardens. The park has water features, flower gardens, walking routes, and covered lounging places, offering a calm ambiance for visitors.

Al-Andalus Botanical Garden: Adjacent to the Al-Andalus Garden Park, the Al-Andalus Botanical Garden shows a large variety of plant species, including fragrant herbs, medicinal plants, and exotic flowers. It acts as a learning center for botanical enthusiasts and wildlife lovers.

Al-Azhar Park Palm Promenade: The Palm Promenade inside Al-Azhar Park provides a calm path surrounded by palm trees, offering shade and a serene ambiance. Visitors may take a leisurely walk, enjoy the fresh air, and admire the park's wonderful architecture.

Al-Andalus Fountain Park: Situated near Cairo International Airport, Al-Andalus Fountain Park is a lovely park containing stunning fountains, vibrant flower beds, and wide green areas. It is a perfect area for a calm stroll or a pleasant lunch.

Al-Azhar Park Viewpoint: Located in Al-Azhar Park, the Viewpoint provides panoramic views of Cairo's cityscape, including prominent buildings such as the Citadel and the Sultan Hassan Mosque. Visitors may enjoy spectacular panoramas while taking in the park's calm ambiance.

Al-Azhar Park Tea Garden: Within Al-Azhar Park, the Tea Garden provides a calm atmosphere where guests may rest, have a cup of tea or coffee, and taste exquisite pastries. The garden's calm ambiance, covered seats, and breathtaking vistas make it an ideal spot to rest and revitalize.

Conclusion: Cairo's parks and gardens give much-needed relief from the city's hustle and bustle, providing tourists an opportunity to reconnect with nature and discover tranquillity. From the ancient Al-Azhar Park to the scenic Gezira Club Park, each green area has its particular charm and charms. Whether you're seeking a leisurely walk, a picnic with loved ones, or a tranquil escape, Cairo's parks and gardens are guaranteed to give an amazing experience, bringing harmony and beauty to the heart of this busy city.

Bruce Terry

BEST NIGHT CLUBS AND BARS IN CAIRO

As the sun sets, Cairo changes into an epicenter for nightlife fans, providing a vast choice of nightclubs and pubs. Whether you're a resident searching for a new hotspot or a tourist seeking an exceptional experience, we have created a list of the 20 greatest nightclubs and bars in Cairo. Each location has its particular character, presenting a broad choice of music, ambiance, and entertainment alternatives.

Cairo Jazz Club: Cairo Jazz Club is a classic institution that has become an iconic location for live music fans. With a calm environment and an amazing roster of local and worldwide jazz performers, this club delivers a memorable experience.

The Tap East: Located in the New Cairo neighborhood, The Tap East is a fashionable pub and live music venue. Its vibrant ambiance, live entertainment, and broad drink menu make it a favorite among residents and tourists alike.

Bus Stop: Situated in the center of Zamalek, Bus Stop is a laid-back tavern with a vintage vibe. Offering a large choice of beers, drinks, and tasty cuisine, it's a fantastic venue for a casual night out.

Sequoia: Nestled on the banks of the Nile River, Sequoia provides a beautiful vista and a classy ambiance. With its outdoor patio and wide menu, including Lebanese and Mediterranean food, it's a great destination for a wonderful evening.

The Lemon Tree & Co: This elegant rooftop bar in Zamalek offers an appealing environment with breathtaking views of Cairo's cityscape. The Lemon Tree & Co. provides a refreshing assortment of beverages and a relaxing ambiance suitable for unwinding.

The Garden Nile Front: As the name implies, this charming location features a stunning garden setting overlooking the Nile River. The Garden Nile Front is recognized for its amazing drinks, live music, and comfortable environment that makes for a pleasant night out.

Roof Bar at Nile Ritz-Carlton: For a premium experience, come to the Roof Bar at Nile Ritz-Carlton. Perched on the hotel's rooftop, this bar provides panoramic views of the city. Sip on excellent drinks while enjoying the classy ambiance.

Zigzag: Zigzag is a prominent nightclub in the middle of Downtown Cairo. Known for its wide music choices, from techno to hip-hop, it draws a diverse population of music aficionados and party-goers.

Cairo Liquor Store: This tiny pub in Zamalek has a lovely speakeasy ambiance. With a professionally chosen drink menu, featuring a large range of spirits and artisan cocktails, Cairo Liquor Store is a sanctuary for mixology fans.

Cairo Capital Club: Located in the Nile City Towers, Cairo Capital Club is an elite venue providing a premium experience. With its contemporary style, rooftop pool, and beautiful views of the Nile, it's a fantastic destination to spend a stylish night out.

Riverside: Situated in Maadi, Riverside is a renowned bar and restaurant noted for its vibrant atmosphere and breathtaking Nile view. Whether you're searching for a calm evening or a night of dancing, Riverside offers it all.

El Villa Zamalek: El Villa Zamalek is a sophisticated club and bar tucked on Zamalek Island. Known for its elegant décor, live DJ performances, and innovative drinks, it's a hip venue frequented by Cairo's fashionable population.

Cavallini: Cavallini, situated in Sheikh Zayed, provides a unique combination of eating, drinking, and live entertainment. With its vast outdoor space and dynamic environment, it's a perfect spot to relax and enjoy a night of fun.

The Tug Boat Lounge: This one-of-a-kind club is set on a converted tugboat on the Nile. The Tug Boat Lounge provides a fascinating experience with its nautical motif, live music, and a varied choice of beverages to pick from.

Bruce Terry

The Tap Maadi: Known for its vibrant environment and active audience, The Tap Maadi is a favorite location for beer connoisseurs. With an enormous range of specialty beers, wonderful cuisine, and frequent live music events, it's constantly humming with activity.

Alchemy: Located in the center of Zamalek, Alchemy is a fashionable cocktail bar noted for its inventive mixology. The bar's talented bartenders produce distinctive and imaginative beverages, making it a must-visit location for cocktail connoisseurs.

Cairo Marriott Hotel Sky Lounge: Perched on the 20th level of the historic Cairo Marriott Hotel, the Sky Lounge provides amazing views of the Nile and the city. With its classy ambiance, live music, and outstanding cocktail selection, it's a great destination for a refined night out.

Graffiti Lounge & Bar: Graffiti Lounge & Bar, located in the Four Seasons Hotel Cairo in Nile Plaza, provides a sophisticated and premium atmosphere. It includes a comprehensive selection of traditional and unique drinks, making it a go-to place for cocktail connoisseurs.

The Cellar Zamalek: Nestled in Zamalek, The Cellar is a subterranean pub noted for its intimate environment and lives music performances. With its large assortment of beers, wines, and spirits, it's a terrific area to relax and enjoy the excellent company.

The Garden Nile Front - Garden City: The Garden Nile Front - Garden City is a sister branch of the famed Garden Nile Front venue. It provides the same spectacular vistas, great music, and wonderful cuisine. This location is situated in the historic Garden City district, giving a bit of elegance to your night out.

Conclusion: Cairo's dynamic nightlife culture provides an astounding choice of nightclubs and bars catering to every taste and inclination. Whether you like jazz, live music, rooftop views, mixology, or just seeking a peaceful ambiance, the 20 locations mentioned above are guaranteed to give an amazing experience. So, put on your dancing shoes, indulge in scrumptious cocktails, and immerse yourself in the exciting atmosphere of Cairo's top nightclubs and pubs.

NIGHTLIFE IN CAIRO

- **ROMANTIC EVENING**

Cairo also has a charming romantic atmosphere that is ideal for creating enduring memories with your special someone. This travel guide will provide you with a thorough schedule to make the most of your romantic evening in Cairo, regardless of whether you're organizing a honeymoon, an anniversary celebration, or just a romantic trip.

Nile River boat: Take a leisurely Nile River boat to start your romantic evening. The serene river current and captivating views of Cairo's skyline combine to create a magnificent atmosphere as the sun starts to set. There are many different types of cruises, from opulent dinner cruises to rustic wooden sailboats called feluccas. Take in the gorgeous views while enjoying a delicious supper on board, live music, and traditional Egyptian entertainment.

Felucca Ride: Select a private felucca ride on the Nile River for a more personal experience. These historic Egyptian sailboats provide a serene and intimate atmosphere, enabling you to take in Cairo's splendor from a new angle.

With your lover by your side, glide down the river as you take in the city's lighted monuments, including the Cairo Tower and downtown Cairo's sparkling lights. Allow the tranquility of the river and the chilly wind to combine to create a really lovely experience.

No trip to Cairo would be complete without taking in the splendor of the Pyramids of Giza's Sound and Light Show. The Sound and Light Show, a captivating audiovisual production that brings the history of the pyramids to life, may enhance the experience. The pyramids are lighted as night falls and a dramatic narrative goes along with the breathtaking visual effects. The majesty of the pyramids, the captivating lights, and the narration all come together to create a truly beautiful and memorable ambiance.

Rooftop eating: Cairo has a thriving eating scene, so what better way to spend a special evening with your significant other than to indulge in a rooftop supper and take in the city's breathtaking scenery? You may enjoy a range of foreign and local cuisines while admiring Cairo's skyline on the rooftops of several hotels and restaurants. You'll discover the ideal place to spend a romantic candlelight meal, from luxury fine dining locations to hip rooftop bars.

Al-Azhar Park: Find peace and quiet here as you flee the city's noise and activity. A hidden treasure in Cairo, this wonderfully designed park provides stunning views of the city's skyline, lush gardens, and tranquil water features. Walk hand in hand along the meandering trails, have a picnic in a quiet area, or just sit back and take in the tranquility. The park's serene surroundings and romantic atmosphere make it the perfect spot to relax and strengthen your relationship.

Cairo's beautiful nightlife combines historical treasures, breathtaking scenery, and a bustling urban environment. Cairo offers a variety of romantic activities that will leave you with

Bruce Terry

lifetime memories, whether you're taking a boat down the Nile, admiring the Pyramids of Giza, or having a rooftop meal. Pack your luggage, go to Egypt, and let Cairo capture your heart as you set off on an incredible romantic journey.

- **LIVE MUSIC**

Genres of Live Music in Cairo: Cairo's music culture is a melting pot of traditional Arabic, Western, and fusion genres. Here are some major genres you might anticipate encountering:

a) *Traditional Arabic Music:* Delve into the enchanting sounds of traditional Arabic music, distinguished by soulful vocalists, sophisticated melodies, and rhythmic rhythms. Traditional instruments such as the oud (lute), qanun (zither), and darbuka (goblet drum) are regularly employed.

b) *Egyptian Shaabi:* Experience the dynamic and addictive rhythms of Egyptian Shaabi, a popular urban folk form that mixes traditional Egyptian music with contemporary influences, typically including electronic elements.

c) *Jazz:* Cairo's jazz culture has been blossoming in recent years, with brilliant local and foreign musicians joining together to produce compelling improvisations and passionate performances.

d) *Rock and Alternative:* Explore the edgier side of Cairo's music scene, with local bands performing rock, alternative, and indie music genres, frequently mixing Western influences with Arabic components.

Top Live Music Places in Cairo:

Cairo is home to several places that exhibit live music performances. Here are some highly suggested ones:

a) *Cairo Opera House:* A prominent cultural institution featuring classical music concerts, opera performances, and symphonic presentations. It also offers current music events and festivals.

b) *El Sawy Culturewheel:* Located on the banks of the Nile, this cultural center provides numerous performance venues, including the River Hall and Wisdom Hall, where you can enjoy live music events spanning diverse genres.

c) *Makan:* A unique venue committed to preserving traditional Arabic music and encouraging cultural interchange. Makan provides small concerts and shows, frequently including local artists and traditional groups.

d) *100Copies Music Space:* This independent music venue encourages experimental and alternative music. It presents frequent live performances by local and international musicians, giving a platform for cutting-edge sounds.

e) *Cairo Jazz Club:* A famous nightlife venue, Cairo Jazz Club provides a broad roster of live music, including jazz, fusion, techno, and more. It highlights both local and international artists, guaranteeing a colorful and energetic environment.

Tips for Enjoying Live Music in Cairo:

To get the most out of your live music experience in Cairo, consider the following tips:

a) *Research Upcoming Events:* Check local event listings, venue websites, and social media channels to keep current on future live music performances and festivals.

b) *Dress Code:* While some venues have a relaxed dress code, some may need a more formal costume, especially for classical music events. It's essential to check the dress code in advance to ensure you are adequately dressed.

c) *Ticket Reservations:* For popular events, it is suggested to reserve tickets in advance to ensure your position. Some venues provide online ticketing, while others may require buying tickets at the door.

d) *Arrive Early:* To acquire the finest seats and completely immerse oneself in the environment, it's essential to arrive early to the venue.

e) *Respect Cultural Norms:* Be conscious of local traditions and decorum during performances. Applauding at suitable moments, abstaining from chatting loudly during performances, and appreciating the artists and other audience members are considered courteous gestures.

Conclusion: Cairo's live music scene is a lively tapestry of varied genres and cultural influences, giving a unique experience for music enthusiasts and tourists alike. Whether you're a lover of traditional Arabic tunes, jazz improvisations, or rock anthems, Cairo's live music venues provide an assortment of alternatives. Immerse yourself in the rich soundtrack of Egypt's capital city, and let the melodies take you through an incredible trip of music and culture.

FESTIVALS AND EVENTS IN CAIRO

Cairo Foreign Film Festival: This yearly event features a broad spectrum of local and foreign films. It gathers prominent directors, actors, and movie aficionados from across the globe.

Cairo International Book Market: Considered the biggest book market in the Arab world, this event brings together publishers, writers, and book enthusiasts. Visitors may peruse a wide collection of books and attend book signings, lectures, and literary conversations.

Bruce Terry

Cairo Jazz event: Jazz fans go to this event to witness live performances by local and international jazz performers. The festival provides a colorful environment, improvisation workshops, and jamming evenings.

Nile Sunset Cruise: An exquisite experience for travelers, a sunset cruise on the Nile River enables you to observe Cairo's skyline while enjoying live music, great cuisine, and traditional entertainment.

Cairo Fashion Festival: Showcasing the newest trends in fashion, this event draws designers, models, and fashion fans. It comprises runway displays, exhibits, and seminars.

Cairo Opera House Summer Festival: Held yearly throughout the summer months, this festival presents a broad schedule of classical music concerts, ballet performances, and theatrical shows.

Egyptian International Modern Dance Festival: Celebrating modern dance, this festival showcases performances by famous dancers and choreographers from Egypt and throughout the globe. Workshops and workshops are also provided for aspiring dancers.

Cairo International Puppet Theater event: This event brings together puppeteers and puppet fans to celebrate the art of puppetry. Performances include classic puppet shows, shadow plays, and experimental puppet theater.

Bruce Terry

Al Moulid Al Nabi: Also known as the Prophet's Birthday, this religious holiday honors the birth of the Islamic prophet Muhammad. It is commemorated with processions, street festivals, and traditional entertainment.

Coptic Christmas: Celebrated by Egypt's Coptic Christian population, Coptic Christmas is a joyful event including church services, traditional processions, and vivid decorations.

Cairo International Book and Author Fair: This event displays the work of local and international writers, publishers, and literary organizations. It provides book signings, panel talks, and seminars on different literary issues.

Cairo International Song event: Dedicated to promoting Arabic music, this event comprises live performances by prominent singers and artists. It comprises tournaments, concerts, and cultural activities.

Cairo Experimental Theater Festival: Emphasizing avant-garde and experimental theater, this festival features unique performances by Egyptian and foreign theatrical organizations. It explores unorthodox ideas and dramatic tactics.

Bruce Terry

Cairo International Festival for Contemporary and Experimental theatrical: This festival focuses on contemporary and experimental theatrical works. It showcases acts that push the limits of conventional theater and question artistic traditions.

Cairo International Biennale for Visual Arts: Showcasing contemporary visual arts, this biannual event draws artists, collectors, and art aficionados. It comprises exhibits, installations, and interactive art experiences.

Cairo International Women's Film Festival: Dedicated to recognizing the work of female filmmakers, this festival plays films made by women from various regions of the globe. It strives to promote gender equality and diversity in the film business.

Cairo International Arabian horse Show: This event combines horse lovers and breeders to highlight the beauty and elegance of Arabian horses. It involves contests, demonstrations, and presentations of these gorgeous creatures.

Cairo International Puppetry Festival: Celebrating the art of puppetry, this festival showcases performances by local and international puppeteers. It gives a place for puppeteers to share ideas, cooperate, and demonstrate their skills.

Bruce Terry

Cairo International Event for Current and Experimental Poetry: This event emphasizes current poetry and experimental forms of literary expression. It features poetry readings, seminars, and talks with prominent poets.

Cairo International Marathon: Athletes and running aficionados participate in this yearly marathon, which takes them past the city's prominent sites. The event emphasizes exercise, community interaction, and a healthy lifestyle.

HEALTH AND SAFETY IN CAIRO

a. *Vaccinations and Medical Preparations:* Before flying to Cairo, it is essential to check with a healthcare expert or a travel medicine specialist to review your health and immunization requirements. The following immunizations are typically recommended for tourists visiting Egypt:

b. *standard vaccines:* Ensure you are up-to-date on standard vaccines such as measles-mumps-rubella (MMR), diphtheria-tetanus-pertussis (DTaP), varicella (chickenpox), and influenza.

c. *Hepatitis A and A*: Consider being vaccinated against hepatitis A and B, since these illnesses can be contracted through contaminated food, water, or close contact with infected persons.

c. *Typhoid:* Since typhoid may be spread by contaminated food and water, particularly in places with inadequate sanitation, it is advised to consider being vaccinated.

d. *Rabies:* Depending on your activities and the length of your stay, you should consider a rabies vaccine, especially if you expect to be in close contact with animals or participate in outdoor activities.

Safe Food and Water:

Maintaining appropriate hygiene and eating safe food and water are vital for keeping healthy while in Cairo. Follow these tips:

a. *Consume Bottled Water:* It is suggested to consume bottled water or water that has been thoroughly treated. Avoid tap water, including ice cubes and drinking water from unknown sources.

c. *Eat at Reputable Establishments*: Choose well-established and reputable restaurants and food sellers to limit the danger of foodborne diseases. Ensure that the dish is prepared completely and served hot.

c. *Wash Hands Frequently:* Wash your hands with soap and clean water before eating or handling food to lower the risk of bacterial and viral illnesses.

Bruce Terry

Heat and Sun Protection:

Cairo receives hot and dry weather throughout the year. Protect yourself from the blazing sun and heat-related illnesses:

a. *Use Sunscreen:* Apply a broad-spectrum sunscreen with a high SPF before venturing out, even on overcast days. Reapply often, particularly after swimming or with intense perspiration.

b. *Dress Appropriately:* Wear lightweight, breathable clothes that cover your skin to defend against sunburn and overheating. For further protection, think about donning a hat and sunglasses.

c. *remain Hydrated:* Drink lots of water to remain hydrated, particularly during hot weather. Bring a reusable water bottle with you and fill it up often.

Transportation Safety:

When touring Cairo, it's necessary to consider transportation safety:

a. *Use Licensed Transportation:* Choose reputed taxi services or ride-hailing apps like Uber and Careem. Verify that the car has correct identification and confirm the driver is using a meter or agree on a fee in advance.

b. *Traffic and Pedestrian Safety:* Cairo's traffic can be hectic, so use caution while crossing the road. Use designated crosswalks and pay attention to traffic signals.

c. *Public Transportation*: The Cairo Metro is a handy and economical form of transit. Be aware of pickpockets and keep your stuff safe.

Security Considerations:

While Cairo is typically secure for visitors, it's vital to be cautious of your surroundings and take precautions:

a. *Be Aware of Scams:* Be careful of people offering unsolicited aid, since they can have hidden motivations. Avoid revealing personal or financial information to unfamiliar persons.

b. *Respect Local Customs*: Familiarize oneself with local customs and traditions to prevent accidentally upsetting people. Dress modestly, especially while visiting religious locations.

c. *Stay Informed:* Stay current on the latest travel warnings and security alerts issued by your government or consulate. Register your trip plans and contact details with your embassy or consulate.

Conclusion: By prioritizing your health and safety, you may completely enjoy your vacation to Cairo. Remember to speak with a healthcare expert before going, adopt healthy eating and water habits, protect yourself from the sun, utilize trustworthy transportation, and be attentive to security risks. With these measures in mind, you may tour Cairo's unique sights and make lasting memories while assuring a safe and pleasurable vacation.

PHARMACY AND FIRST AID

When going on a voyage to Cairo, Egypt, it is vital to be prepared for any unanticipated events. Familiarizing oneself with the local pharmacies and first aid facilities can bring a piece of mind and safeguard your safety and well-being during your vacation. In this tutorial, we will cover the significance of pharmacies and first aid in Cairo, along with recommendations on finding them and dealing with typical health difficulties.

Understanding the Importance of Pharmacies and First Aid in *Cairo*: Cairo is a dynamic and busy city with a rich cultural legacy. However, like any other tourist site, travelers may suffer health difficulties or small mishaps during their stay. Pharmacies and first aid clinics play a significant role in providing rapid medical help, dispensing required drugs, and giving expert advice on health-related matters.

Locating Pharmacies:

a. *Egyptian Red Crescent Society:* The Egyptian Red Crescent Society maintains various pharmacies across Cairo. They are recognized for their dependability and availability of a broad selection of drugs. You may locate their branches in key places, near large hospitals, and in important tourist spots.

b. *Chain Pharmacies:* Cairo is home to numerous well-known pharmacy chains, including El Ezaby Pharmacy and Seif Pharmacies. These businesses have branches dispersed over the city and provide 24-hour services in numerous areas. Look for their recognized emblems or ask locals for instructions.

c. *Local Pharmacies:* In addition to chain pharmacies, Cairo has several independent pharmacies that cater to the requirements of the local population. These tiny pharmacies may be located in residential areas and near marketplaces. While they may have limited English-speaking employees, they frequently give individualized care and have a solid assortment of popular prescriptions.

Essential First Aid Tips:

a. *Basic First Aid Knowledge:* It is advised that travelers have basic first aid knowledge to treat minor injuries or illnesses. Familiarize yourself with methods such as CPR, wound treatment, and bandaging. Online resources and first aid classes might be valuable for obtaining these abilities.

b. *Carry a First Aid Kit:* Pack a well-stocked first aid kit with products like sticky bandages, antiseptic wipes, painkillers, antihistamines, and any personal drugs you need. This will help you to manage minor problems swiftly.

Common Health Concerns and Remedies:

a. *Traveler's Diarrhea:* The change in water and diet might create stomach troubles. Stay hydrated, avoid tap water, and drink only bottled water. Over-the-counter drugs like loperamide (Imodium) may give relief, but visit a pharmacist or a healthcare practitioner if symptoms continue.

b. *Sunburn and Heat Exhaustion:* Cairo's environment may be hot, so protect yourself from the heat by wearing a hat, applying sunscreen, and finding shade when required. Stay hydrated and search for air-conditioned locations to prevent heat fatigue.

b. *Respiratory Issues:* Cairo's air quality may offer issues for those with respiratory ailments. If you have a pre-existing ailment, ensure you have an appropriate supply of drugs and consider using a mask as required.

Conclusion: Prioritizing your health and well-being when traveling is crucial, and being informed of the pharmacy and first aid choices in Cairo will help you face any unforeseen problems. Remember to find pharmacies in advance, carry a well-equipped first aid kit, and

Bruce Terry

be acquainted with basic first aid methods. By following these instructions, you may enjoy your stay in Cairo with confidence, knowing that you are prepared to manage any health issues that may emerge.

CHAPTER 7

FOOD AND DRINK

- ### LOCAL DRINKS

Cairo, the energetic capital of Egypt, is renowned for its varied and savory local drinks in addition to its glorious monuments and rich history. Cairo provides a beautiful selection of beverages that perfectly represent the spirit of Egyptian culture, ranging from revitalizing fruit juices to conventional herbal teas. We shall examine 20 typical Cairo beverages in this post, emphasizing their cultural relevance, ingredients, and methods of preparation.

Karkadeh: Karkadeh is a popular Egyptian drink made from hibiscus blossoms. The dried petals are brewed to produce a brilliant crimson infusion with a tart, cranberry-like taste. Karkadeh is typically consumed both hot and cold and is noted for its refreshing and cooling characteristics.

Sahlab: Sahlab is a warm and creamy beverage prepared from orchid tubers, milk, and sugar, and sweetened with flavors like cinnamon and coconut. Served warm, this rich and velvety drink is especially popular throughout the winter months.

Tamr Hindi: Tamr Hindi, also known as Tamarind juice, is a tangy and sweet drink produced from tamarind pulp, sugar, and water.

This delicious beverage delivers a unique blend of tastes and is great for relieving your thirst on a hot Cairo day.

Sobia: Sobia is a classic Egyptian drink prepared from rice, coconut milk, and sugar. This creamy mixture is commonly scented with rosewater or orange blossom water, giving it a delicate and aromatic taste. Sobia is often served cold and is a favorite during Ramadan.

Qamar al-Din: Qamar al-Din is a rich apricot nectar produced from dried apricot paste. This famous Ramadan drink is praised both for its rich taste and its nutritious content. Qamar al-Din is often diluted with water before drinking.

Mango Juice: Egypt is famed for its delicious and juicy mangoes, and the mango juice in Cairo is no exception. Freshly squeezed mango juice gives a rush of tropical taste and is a favorite option among residents and visitors alike.

Sugar Cane Juice: Sugar cane juice is a delicious and natural drink that can be obtained on Cairo's crowded streets. Made by pressing the sugarcane stalks, this sweet and hydrating beverage is typically sweetened with a splash of lime or ginger for extra flavor.

Sakkara: Sakkara is a unique drink that mixes tastes from different fruits and plants. This bright combination is produced by combining bananas, dates, honey, milk, almonds, and a dash of cinnamon. Sakkara is a creamy and healthy solution for people seeking a delicious drink.

Carob Juice: Carob juice is a nutritious beverage prepared from the pods of the carob tree. The pods are crushed into a powder and combined with milk or water to make a naturally sweet and chocolaty drink. Carob juice is widely appreciated as a healthier alternative to cocoa-based beverages.

Licorice Tea: Licorice tea, also known as "erk-soos" in Egypt, is a popular herbal infusion with a peculiar taste. Made from the roots of the licorice plant, this tea has a naturally sweet flavor and is thought to improve digestion and relieve sore throats.

Mint Lemonade: Mint lemonade is a typical Egyptian drink that mixes freshly squeezed lemon juice, mint leaves, sugar, and water. This invigorating and zesty beverage gives a cooling effect and is especially relished during the warm summer months.

Tamarind Shake: Tamarind shake is a rich and velvety drink created with tamarind pulp, milk, sugar, and ice. This creamy mixture delivers a lovely blend of acidic and sweet tastes and is a fantastic treat for dessert or a hot day.

Hibiscus Lemonade: Hibiscus lemonade is a delightful variation of the standard lemonade. It mixes the acidity of hibiscus blossoms with the zesty taste of lemon juice, resulting in a lively and thirst-quenching drink that is sometimes topped with mint leaves.

Mulberry Juice: Mulberry juice is a rich and sweet beverage prepared from the ripe berries of the mulberry tree. The rich purple juice has a natural sweetness and is loved for its unusual taste and possible health advantages.

Tamarind Date Juice: Tamarind date juice is a wonderful combination of tamarind pulp, dates, sugar, and water. This sweet and tangy drink delivers a balanced blend of tastes and is widely drunk throughout Ramadan for its revitalizing benefits.

White Coffee: White coffee, also known as "Sada al-bouna," is a classic Egyptian drink prepared from lightly roasted coffee beans. Unlike the black and powerful flavor of ordinary coffee, white coffee has a softer taste and is commonly served with sugar or sweet spices like cardamom.

Jallab: Jallab is a popular drink during Ramadan and other special occasions. Made from grape molasses, rose water, and a combination of other nuts, jallab has a rich and sweet taste profile that is often poured over crushed ice.

Amar al-Din: Amar al-Din is a pleasant apricot nectar that is popularly loved in Cairo. Made from dried apricot paste, this drink is generally diluted with water and served chilled. Its acidic and fruity flavor makes it a pleasant option on a hot day.

Saffron Milk: Saffron milk is a rich and fragrant drink produced by infusing milk with saffron threads and sweetening it with sugar or honey. This decadent beverage is recognized for its vivid yellow hue and subtle floral taste.

Egyptian Tea: Egyptian tea, or "shai," is a common drink in Cairo. Traditionally served black with a side of sugar cubes, this powerful and robust tea is prepared to perfection and is typically enjoyed at social events or as a calming companion to a savory dinner.

Conclusion: Cairo's native beverages provide a broad spectrum of tastes and textures, each adding to Egypt's unique culinary tapestry. Whether you favor refreshing fruit juices, calming herbal infusions, or creamy concoctions, Cairo's beverage scene offers something to suit every pallet. So, the next time you find yourself in this busy metropolis, don't miss the chance to experience the rich world of Cairo's native beverages and delight in the real flavors of Egypt.

Bruce Terry

- **STREET FOODS**

Exploring the busy streets of Cairo provides a choice of scrumptious delicacies that represent the city's culinary history. From spicy nibbles to sweet pleasures, here are 20 must-try street delicacies in Cairo that will excite your taste buds and give you a genuine feel of the city.

Kushari: Considered the national meal of Egypt, Kushari is a substantial blend of pasta, grains, lentils, chickpeas, and crispy fried onions, topped with tangy tomato sauce and spicy garlic vinegar. This tasty and budget-friendly street cuisine can be found at practically every corner of Cairo.

Falafel: Egyptian falafel, known as ta'ameya, is produced with ground fava beans combined with herbs and spices before being deep-fried to perfection. Served in warm pita bread with tahini sauce and fresh veggies, these crispy and savory falafels are a must-try.

Koshary Pancake: A new take on the original kushari, the koshary pancake mixes the tastes of the renowned street dish with a pancake-like foundation. Topped with kushari ingredients and wrapped into a wonderful savory pancake, this unusual concoction is a real Cairo specialty.

Ful Medames: A classic Egyptian morning staple, ful medames consists of slow-cooked fava beans combined with olive oil, lemon juice, and a variety of spices. Served with a piece of freshly made bread, this healthful and tasty meal is a terrific way to start your day.

Hawawshi: Hawawshi is an Egyptian meat pie prepared of minced meat (typically beef or lamb), combined with onions, bell peppers, and a mixture of spices. The meat mixture is then placed into a pocket of baladi bread and cooked until brown and crispy. Hawawshi is a wonderful and gratifying street snack that is appreciated by residents and tourists alike.

Shawarma: A famous Middle Eastern street snack, shawarma has also earned its way into the hearts (and stomachs) of Cairo's citizens. Thinly sliced marinated meat, generally chicken or beef, is roasted on a vertical spit and then wrapped in warm pita bread with garlic sauce, tahini, and a variety of vegetables.

Sambusak: Similar to samosas, sambusak is a delicious pastry filled with different components such as spiced ground beef, cheese, or vegetables. These bite-sized delicacies are deep-fried to perfection, making them a favorite street food snack in Cairo.

Fatteh: Fatteh is a decadent meal composed of layers of toasted pita bread, cooked chickpeas, yogurt, and garlic. It is then drizzled with melted butter and dusted with a combination of spices. This creamy and savory meal is a lovely blend of textures and tastes.

Feteer Meshaltet: Feteer Meshaltet is a flaky and buttery Egyptian pastry that comes in both sweet and savory variants. The sweet variety is commonly filled with honey, almonds, and cinnamon, while the savory one might be packed with cheese, sausage, or a mix of components. Feteer Meshaltet is a must-try for pastry enthusiasts.

Molokhia: Molokhia is a classic Egyptian soup produced from the leaves of the molokhia plant, which gives the dish its unique green hue. The leaves are coarsely chopped and sautéed with garlic and coriander, then served with soft pieces of chicken or rabbit, accompanied with rice or toast.

Qatayef: Qatayef is a favorite sweet delicacy during the month of Ramadan. These little pancakes are filled with a variety of tasty ingredients, such as almonds, cheese, or cream. They are then deep-fried till crispy and served with a sprinkling of sugar syrup.

Konafa: Konafa is a typical Egyptian delicacy created with thin strands of pastry dough covered with sweet cheese or almonds. This delectable dessert is roasted till golden and crispy and then immersed in a fragrant sugar syrup. Konafa is commonly savored during festive events and is a genuine luxury.

Basbousa: Basbousa is a semolina cake steeped in sugar syrup and flavored with rosewater or orange blossom water. This rich and moist cake is sometimes topped with nuts, making it a sweet and fragrant treat that is much liked in Cairo.

Foul: Foul is a traditional Egyptian street snack prepared from fava beans, which are boiled until soft and mashed, then blended with olive oil, lemon juice, and spices. Served with a piece of freshly baked bread, foul is a wholesome and delightful alternative for breakfast or lunch.

Ro'aak: Ro'aak is a wonderful Egyptian street snack made from layers of filo pastry packed with a sweet nut filling. These compact, bite-sized pastries are deep-fried till golden and crispy and then coated with powdered sugar. Ro'aak is a fantastic treat for individuals with a sweet craving.

Kofta Sandwich: Kofta sandwiches are a popular street food alternative in Cairo. Grilled or roasted ground meat, generally beef or lamb, is seasoned with herbs and spices, then wrapped in warm pita bread with tahini sauce, tomatoes, onions, and parsley. The outcome is a rich and enjoyable dinner on the road.

Luqaimat: Luqaimat are little, deep-fried dough balls that are popular during Ramadan and other festive occasions. These bite-sized snacks are crispy on the exterior, soft on the inside, and are

Bruce Terry

generally drizzled with honey or sugar syrup, making them a pleasant sweet pleasure.

Grilled Corn: Grilled corn is a simple but excellent street meal available in Cairo. Corn on the cob is cooked over hot charcoal until the kernels are soft and slightly browned. It is then coated with butter and dusted with salt and spices, giving a delightful and fulfilling snack.

Alexandrian Liver: Alexandrian liver, or kibda Iskandarani, is a famous street food delicacy that originated in Alexandria but can be found in Cairo as well. Thinly sliced calf or lamb liver is sautéed with onions, garlic, and a combination of spices until soft and delicious. Served with a side of bread, this meal is a favorite among liver aficionados.

Baladi Bread and Cheese: Sometimes, simplicity is paramount, and the combination of baladi bread and cheese is a testimony to that. Baladi bread, a typical Egyptian flatbread, is commonly served with a variety of local cheeses, such as mish or rumi, delivering a fast and tasty snack that is appreciated by Cairo's people.

Conclusion: Cairo's street food culture is a real representation of the city's rich culinary legacy. Exploring the colorful alleys of Cairo will present you with a broad choice of scrumptious foods,

Bruce Terry

from classic Egyptian favorites to creative inventions. Whether you're a lover of spicy pleasures like kushari and falafel or have a sweet desire for goodies like konafa and qatayef, the street food of Cairo guarantees to fulfill your demands and give an amazing gourmet experience

Bruce Terry

CHAPTER 8

TRAVELING ITINERARY

CAIRO TRAVEL ITINERARY FOR 3 DAYS

- **Day 1: Exploring Ancient Egypt**

Morning:

Start your day by seeing the Giza Plateau, situated on the outskirts of Cairo. This UNESCO World Heritage Site is home to the renowned Great Pyramids of Giza, including the Great Pyramid of Khufu, the Pyramid of Khafre, and the Pyramid of Menkaure. Marvel at the towering buildings that have lasted the test of time for almost 4,500 years and learn about the ancient Egyptian civilization.

Adjacent to the pyramids, you'll discover the renowned Sphinx, a colossal figure with the body of a lion and the head of a pharaoh. Take some time to examine this old structure and get amazing images.

After seeing the pyramids, visit the neighboring Solar Boat Museum, where you can see the surprisingly well-preserved Khufu Ship, an ancient Egyptian watercraft unearthed near the Great Pyramid. The museum gives unique insights into ancient Egyptian boat-building processes and their relevance in the afterlife.

Bruce Terry

Afternoon:

Head back to downtown Cairo and visit the Egyptian Museum, situated in Tahrir Square. This world-renowned museum holds a significant collection of ancient Egyptian antiquities, including the treasures of Tutankhamun, mummies, sculptures, and jewelry. Spend a few hours examining the numerous exhibitions and immerse yourself in the enthralling history of Egypt.

For lunch, try authentic Egyptian food at a nearby eatery. Try foods like koshari (a blend of grains, lentils, and pasta), falafel, and shawarma.

Evening:

As the sun sets, enjoy a pleasant felucca boat ride down the Nile River. Enjoy the quiet environment and amazing views of Cairo's skyline. You may also choose an evening cruise to enjoy a superb meal while being entertained by live music and traditional Egyptian dance displays.

After the boat journey, proceed to Khan El Khalili, one of Cairo's oldest and most renowned marketplaces. This lively market provides a dynamic shopping experience, with stores offering spices, jewelry, textiles, and souvenirs. Explore the small alleyways, haggle for prices, and take up the bustling atmosphere before returning to your lodgings.

- **Day 2: Islamic Cairo and Coptic Cairo**

Morning:

Begin your second day with a tour of the ancient quarter of Islamic Cairo. Start with the Citadel of Saladin, an ancient fortification that gives panoramic views of the city. Inside the citadel, you'll discover the spectacular Mosque of Muhammad Ali, popularly known as the Alabaster Mosque. Explore its finely crafted interior and learn about its importance in Egyptian history.

From the citadel, make your way to the Sultan Hassan Mosque and the Al-Rifa'i Mosque, both architectural wonders showing beautiful Islamic style. Admire the beautiful intricacies of the domes, minarets, and courtyard while getting insight into Egypt's Islamic past.

Afternoon:

After exploring Islamic Cairo, proceed to Coptic Cairo, the historic Christian section of the city. Begin your trip in the Coptic Museum, which displays a significant collection of Christian antiquities, including ancient texts, icons, and textiles.

Continue to the Hanging Church (Saint Virgin Mary's Coptic Orthodox Church), one of Cairo's oldest and most prominent churches. Marvel at its gorgeous oak ceiling and old iconography.

Next, visit the Ben Ezra Synagogue, situated close. It is considered to be the spot where infant Moses was discovered and has enormous historical importance for both Jews and Christians.

Evening:

For the evening, indulge in Egyptian street cuisine at one of the neighborhood cafés. Try popular delicacies like ful medames (mashed fava beans), taameya (Egyptian falafel), and grilled kebabs.

After supper, proceed to the Sound and Light Show at the Pyramids of Giza. This captivating multimedia event takes you on a trip through ancient Egyptian history, bringing the pyramids and Sphinx to life with breathtaking visual effects and narrative.

- **Day 3: Modern Cairo and Cultural Experiences**

Morning:

Begin your day by touring the bustling district of Zamalek, an island situated in the Nile River. Take a leisurely stroll through the green lanes, explore art galleries, and eat a good breakfast at one of the quaint cafés in the neighborhood.

Afterward, visit the Cairo Opera House, a spectacular cultural facility that presents numerous acts, including ballet, opera, and classical music concerts. Check the schedule in advance to see if any shows fit with your visit.

Afternoon:

Make your way to the lively sector of Downtown Cairo, noted for its architectural treasures from the early 20th century. Walk through the vast boulevards and visit prominent sights such as the Egyptian Museum of Modern Art and the Qasr El Nil Bridge.

For lunch, enjoy Egyptian street cuisine specialties like kofta sandwiches, shawarma, and grilled fish at one of the local street sellers or tiny eateries.

Evening:

End your vacation with a visit to Al-Azhar Park, a beautifully planted green area in the middle of Cairo. Enjoy a leisurely walk around the gardens, appreciating the quiet ambiance and admiring the breathtaking views of the city skyline.

In the evening, consider witnessing a traditional Egyptian music and dance performance. Cairo is home to several venues that feature Egyptian traditional music, belly dance, and Sufi whirling dervishes. Immerse yourself in the colorful rhythms and mesmerizing performances that illustrate Egypt's rich cultural history.

Bruce Terry

This itinerary gives a complete overview of Cairo's historical, cultural, and contemporary attractions, enabling you to enjoy the city's many offerings in only three days. Remember to verify the opening hours and availability of attractions in advance, as well as any travel warnings or restrictions that may be in place.

CAIRO TRAVEL ITINERARY FOR 7 DAYS

- ### Day 1: Arrival and Exploring Islamic Cairo

Start your Cairo experience by landing at Cairo International Airport and settling into your accommodation.

After settling in, travel to Islamic Cairo, a historic region noted for its spectacular mosques and ancient architecture.

Visit the majestic Mosque of Muhammad Ali, better known as the Alabaster Mosque, situated inside the Citadel of Saladin. Take in the magnificent views of the city from the citadel.

Explore the neighboring Sultan Hassan Mosque and the Al-Rifa'i Mosque, both recognized for their stunning architecture and complex embellishments.

End your day with a visit to the Khan El Khalili Bazaar, one of the oldest and most renowned marketplaces in the Middle East. Enjoy shopping for souvenirs, spices, jewelry, and traditional handicrafts.

- **Day 2: Giza Plateau and Egyptian Museum**

Start your day early and make your way to the Giza Plateau to observe the renowned Pyramids of Giza, including the Great Pyramid of Khufu, the Pyramid of Khafre, and the Pyramid of Menkaure. Don't miss the Sphinx, a fabled monster with the head of a human and the body of a lion.

Explore the Solar Watercraft Museum to witness the well-preserved ancient Egyptian watercraft that was unearthed near the Great Pyramid.

Afterward, visit the Egyptian Museum in Tahrir Square, home to an enormous collection of ancient antiquities, including the treasures of Tutankhamun. Marvel at the mummies and learn about the fascinating history of ancient Egypt.

Day 3: Coptic Cairo and Old Cairo

Begin your day by exploring Coptic Cairo, an area noted for its Christian past.

Explore the Hanging Church (Saint Virgin Mary's Coptic Orthodox Church), one of the oldest churches in Egypt, and see its stunning paintings and wooden pulpit.

Visit the Coptic Museum nearby to learn more about Coptic history and explore its magnificent collection of religious art and artifacts.

Continue to Old Cairo and tour the Ben Ezra Synagogue and the Church of St. Sergius and Bacchus, both major religious monuments with intriguing histories.

Take a quiet walk down the tiny alleyways of Old Cairo and absorb the distinct ambiance of this old district.

Day 4: Day Trip to Alexandria

Take a day excursion to the seaside city of Alexandria, just a few hours away from Cairo.

Start by visiting the Qaitbay Citadel, a 15th-century stronghold erected on the site of the historic Lighthouse of Alexandria. Enjoy spectacular views of the Mediterranean Sea from the citadel.

Explore the Catacombs of Kom El Shoqafa, a subterranean burial complex dating back to the Roman Empire.

Visit the beautiful Alexandria Library, one of the most renowned libraries in the ancient world. Admire its contemporary architectural architecture and discover its large collection of books and manuscripts.

Take a leisurely stroll along the Corniche, a lovely waterfront promenade, and enjoy the views of the sea.

Day 5: Memphis, Saqqara, and Dahshur

Embark on a day excursion to discover the ancient ruins of Memphis, Saqqara, and Dahshur, situated on the outskirts of Cairo.

Start with the open-air museum in Memphis, the ancient capital of Egypt, and view the huge statue of Ramses II and other archaeological artifacts.

Continue to Saqqara and view the Step Pyramid of Djoser, the oldest pyramid in Egypt and a UNESCO World Heritage Site. Explore the complex and marvel at its architectural importance.

End your day by visiting Dahshur, where you can witness the Bent Pyramid and the Red Pyramid, both erected during the time of Pharaoh Sneferu. Climb inside the Red Pyramid for a unique experience.

Day 6: Nile River Cruise and Sound and Light Show

Enjoy a calm Nile River cruise and explore Cairo from a fresh viewpoint. Choose from a range of alternatives, such as a lunch cruise or a romantic evening cruise, and eat exquisite Egyptian food while viewing the city's cityscape.

Bruce Terry

In the evening, witness the Sound and Light Show at the Pyramids of Giza. This stunning multimedia display brings the ancient history of Egypt to life via lights, music, and narrative, producing a fascinating experience.

Day 7: Free Day and Departure

Spend your final day in Cairo at your leisure. You may revisit your favorite locations, explore local markets, or indulge in Egyptian cuisine.

If time allows, you may also take a short trip to see the Saladin Citadel or explore the lively streets of Downtown Cairo.

In the evening, check out from your accommodation and go to Cairo International Airport for your departure, waving farewell to the intriguing metropolis of Cairo.

Remember to verify the opening hours and any entrance requirements for the attractions you want to visit. It's also advisable to hire a competent guide or take a guided tour for a greater understanding of Cairo's history and culture. Enjoy your 7-day adventure in Cairo and make lasting memories of this beautiful city!

Bruce Terry

CHAPTER 9

TRAVELLING TO CAIRO DURING RAMADAN

Understanding Ramadan: Ramadan is the ninth month of the Islamic lunar calendar and is considered the holiest month for Muslims. During this period, Muslims practice fasting from sunrise to sunset, refraining from food, drink, smoking, and other bodily requirements. It is a time of introspection, prayer, charity, and family togetherness. Understanding the importance of Ramadan can help you understand and respect the local customs and traditions while visiting Cairo.

Joyous vibe: Cairo during Ramadan emits a distinct and joyous vibe. The streets come alive after dusk, with family and friends gathering for "Iftar," the evening meal to break the fast. The city's busiest marketplaces, such as Khan El Khalili, are covered with exquisite Ramadan decorations, and the perfume of traditional foods fills the air. Take the chance to immerse yourself in this joyous environment and observe the local traditions firsthand.

Prayer & Worship: Islam is profoundly established in Egyptian culture, and Cairo features several gorgeous mosques. The most renowned one is the Al-Azhar Mosque, which is not only an architectural beauty but also a major center for Islamic scholarship. Take the time to visit these mosques, but remember to dress modestly and act properly during prayer times. Non-Muslims are often not permitted inside mosques during prayer, but you may enjoy their magnificence from the outside.

Sightseeing in Cairo: While certain tourist attractions may have adjusted working hours during Ramadan, Cairo's key monuments and historical sites remain available for tourists. Take the chance to tour the Giza Plateau and experience the awe-inspiring Great Pyramids and the Sphinx. The Egyptian Museum, home to an enormous collection of ancient antiquities, is also a must-visit. It's advised to organize your touring excursions early in the day before the heat and fasting hours take their toll.

Etiquette & Respect: Respecting local customs and traditions is vital while visiting Cairo during Ramadan. It's crucial to dress modestly, especially while attending religious locations or public venues. Avoid eating, drinking, or smoking in public during fasting hours out of respect for people observing Ramadan. While restaurants and cafés catering to visitors may be open, it's respectful to enjoy your meals inside or in specified places.

Iftar and Suhoor Experience: Participating in a genuine Iftar or Suhoor experience is highly recommended during your vacation to Cairo. Numerous hotels, restaurants, and local venues provide special Ramadan dinners, enabling you to enjoy authentic Egyptian food and absorb the local traditions. Sharing an Iftar dinner with locals may give great insights into their culture and hospitality. It's essential to make reservations in advance since some establishments might become packed during Ramadan.

Shopping Opportunities: Ramadan is also a fantastic time for shopping in Cairo. The city's bustling marketplaces, such as Khan El Khalili and the City Stars Mall, provide a broad variety of merchandise, including traditional handicrafts, textiles, spices, and jewelry. Take the chance to acquire unique items and immerse yourself in the local shopping experience. Remember to negotiate rates nicely and be careful of merchants who may be observing fasting.

Conclusion: Traveling to Cairo during Ramadan gives a one-of-a-kind cultural experience. Immerse yourself in the festive mood, observe local traditions, and discover the city's intriguing sites. By knowing and recognizing the importance of Ramadan, you may enjoy a respectful and enlightening experience in Cairo, building memories that will last a lifetime.

Bruce Terry

WHAT NOT TO BRING TO CAIRO

To guarantee a successful and comfortable journey to Cairo, it's crucial to think about what goods you should leave behind when you prepare for your vacation. What not to bring to Cairo will be highlighted in this travel guide along with information on regional customs, security issues, and practical considerations.

Excessive Valuables: While it's a good idea to be cautious with your possessions wherever you travel, it's crucial in Cairo. Don't bring a lot of jewelry, an expensive watch, or bright accessories since they could draw unwelcome attention. It's advisable to leave valuables at home or to keep them locked up in the safe at your hotel.

Excessive Cash: It's never a good idea to carry a lot of cash, and Cairo is no exception. The best practice is to withdraw or convert money in tiny amounts as required, even while ATMs and currency exchange services are accessible. When feasible, use safe payment options like credit cards; have a small amount of cash on hand for unforeseen needs.

Cairo is a Muslim-dominated city, therefore it's crucial to follow local traditions and dress modestly. When visiting places of worship or conservative areas, stay away from carrying exposing apparel like short shorts, miniskirts, or low-cut shirts. Instead, choose lightweight, loose-fitting clothing that covers your legs and shoulders.

Uncomfortable Shoes: Cairo exploration often entails a lot of walking; therefore it's essential to carry comfortable shoes. Choose sturdy walking shoes or sandals over high heels or footwear that is unsuitable for extended walks on uneven sidewalks. You may be certain that you can do this while taking in the city's attractions.

Devices that aren't absolutely necessary: Although it's customary to carry devices like cameras, tablets, and cell phones, it's advisable to leave unneeded equipment at home. Carrying many pricey items might raise the possibility of theft or loss. As you do bring gadgets, keep them safe and keep them hidden as possible, especially in busy places.

Without Proper Documentation, Prescription prescriptions: It's crucial to carry prescription prescriptions with you if you need them. Make sure you have copies of your prescriptions and a note from your doctor outlining the reasons why the medicine is necessary for you. Any issues with municipal or customs authorities will be lessened as a result.

Non-essential Travel Documents: In order to prevent theft or loss while touring Cairo, it is advisable to just bring what is required. Keep a photocopy or digital copy of your identifying papers and

Bruce Terry

leave your passport and other vital documents in the hotel safe. Keep your cash to a minimum and simply bring a copy of your travel insurance.

Unfamiliar Foods and Drinks: Cairo has a broad selection of delectable local cuisine, but it's important to use caution while tasting new foods and beverages, particularly street food. Stick to bottled water, eat at reputable establishments, and make sure that any fruits or veggies you ingest are well-cleaned and peeled to prevent any stomach problems or foodborne infections.

In conclusion, you may improve your travel experience and guarantee a secure and pleasurable vacation by being aware of what not to bring to Cairo. Respecting regional traditions, taking care of possessions, and dressing correctly can help you blend in and take in this lovely city's rich cultural legacy. As you tour the energetic streets of Cairo, keep in mind that your comfort, safety, and cultural sensitivity should come first.

Bruce Terry

CONCLUSION

In conclusion, the Egypt Travel Guide for 2023-2024 provides a thorough and enjoyable experience for tourists looking to see this historic and enchanting nation. With its rich historical monuments, gorgeous landscapes, and lively culture, Egypt continues to be a favorite destination for travelers from across the globe.

The book gives useful information on must-visit monuments, such as the magnificent Pyramids of Giza, the famous Sphinx, and the interesting Valley of the Kings. It also showcases lesser-known beauties like the temples of Luxor and Karnak, the lovely alleyways of Alexandria, and the peaceful beaches of the Red Sea.

Travelers may anticipate an immersive voyage through time, where they can observe the relics of one of the world's earliest civilizations. The book gives insights into the history, mythology, and archaeology of Egypt, helping tourists to fully comprehend the importance of the sites they see.

Moreover, the book gives practical ideas and recommendations for a seamless and happy travel experience. It covers themes like transit alternatives, housing, local traditions, and food, ensuring that tourists have all the required knowledge to traverse the nation easily.

Bruce Terry

Additionally, the book highlights the need for responsible tourism, asking travelers to protect Egypt's cultural legacy and natural environment. It supports sustainable practices and proposes strategies to reduce the effect on historical monuments and vulnerable ecosystems.

With the Egypt Travel Guide for 2023-2024 in hand, tourists may embark on a voyage of discovery and wonder. Whether it's seeing ancient monuments, sailing down the Nile, diving in the Red Sea, or immersing one in the bustling marketplaces and bazaars, Egypt guarantees an amazing trip for everyone who comes.

Plan your vacation intelligently, immerse yourself in the rich history and culture, and make experiences that will last a lifetime in the timeless nation of Egypt.

Printed in Great Britain
by Amazon